TROUT-FISHING
the
John Muir Trail

CHARLES S. BECK

Frank
Amato
PORTLAND

About the Author

This is Steve Beck's second fishing guide book, his first was *Yosemite Trout Fishing Guide*, published in 1995. He's a freelance writer, and regularly presents slide shows to fishing clubs. Steve has fly-fished the Sierra for twenty years from his home in Merced (The Gateway to Yosemite), California, where he lives with his wife and two young children.

Like John Muir, and so many others, Steve's first encounter with the Sierra Nevada was in Yosemite National Park. He was so enamored with it that he wanted to see more of the mountain range that Muir called, "...surely the brightest and best of all the Lord has built."

After devoting many years to becoming intimately acquainted with Yosemite and its trout, he turned his attention to the spectacular high country of the southern Sierra. During the past few years, Steve's summers have been pleasurably spent hiking the John Muir Trail, with fly rod in hand, exploring its scenic waters. Of his work on both books he says, "Fishing for the most beautiful fish I know, in the most beautiful place I know, has been a labor of love."

All inquiries should be addressed to:
Frank Amato Publications, Inc.
P.O. Box 82112 • Portland, Oregon 97282
503-653-8108 • www.amatobooks.com

Book Design: Amy Tomlinson
Photography: Steve Beck, unless otherwise noted
Maps: Steve Beck

Printed in Hong Kong
3 5 7 9 10 8 6 4 2

Softbound ISBN: 1-57188-188-3   Softbound UPC: 0-66066-00399-7

CONTENTS

Dedication

For our daughter Maggie,
who saw the first few miles of the John Muir Trail
at six months old while riding on my back.
I'm looking forward to showing her more
of the trail in the coming years.

Acknowledgments

I want to thank the people who contributed to the completion of this book. I received diligent assistance in gathering historical trout stocking information from Melanie Ruesch, Museum Technician, Sequoia and Kings Canyon National Parks, and John Kleinfelter and Curtis Milliron, California Department of Fish and Game Fishery Biologists. Thanks to Dr. Tom Fife, whom I supply with the trout flies that keep him fishing, while he supplies me with the exceptional medical advice that keeps me fishing. Special thanks to my wife, Beth, who patiently endured my time away from the family whether I was deep in the backcountry surrounded by mountains, or deep in thought surrounded by notes at my desk.

THE JOHN MUIR TRAIL

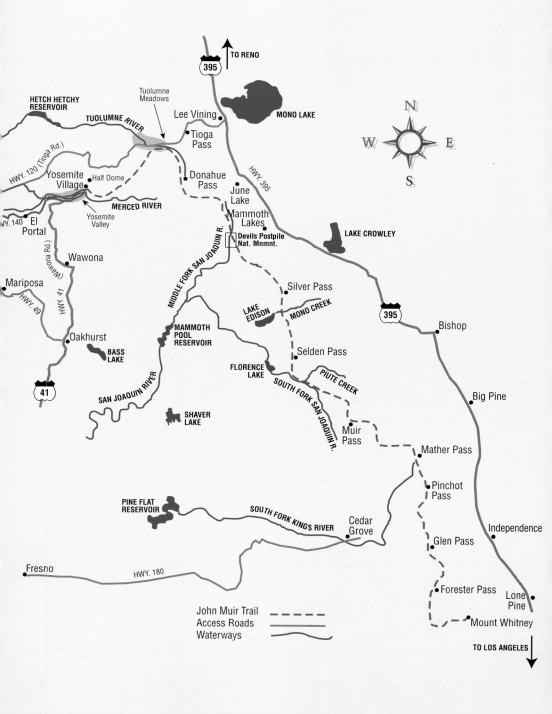

TO RENO

395

HETCH HETCHY
RESERVOIR

TUOLUMNE RIVER

Tuolumne
Meadows

Lee Vining

MONO LAKE

Tioga
Pass

HWY. 120 (Tioga Rd.)

Yosemite
Village

Half Dome

Donahue
Pass

June
Lake

HWY. 395

MERCED RIVER

Yosemite
Valley

HWY. 140

El
Portal

Mammoth
Lakes

Devils Postpile
Nat. Mnmnt.

LAKE CROWLEY

Wawona

(Wawona Rd.)

MIDDLE FORK SAN JOAQUIN R.

HWY. 41

Mariposa

HWY. 49

Silver Pass

LAKE
EDISON

MONO CREEK

395

Bishop

MAMMOTH
POOL
RESERVOIR

Selden Pass

Oakhurst

BASS
LAKE

FLORENCE
LAKE

PIUTE CREEK

41

SAN JOAQUIN RIVER

SOUTH FORK SAN JOAQUIN R.

Big Pine

SHAVER
LAKE

Muir
Pass

Mather Pass

Pinchot
Pass

PINE FLAT
RESERVOIR

SOUTH FORK KINGS RIVER

Cedar
Grove

Independence

Glen Pass

Fresno

HWY. 180

Forester Pass

Lone
Pine

John Muir Trail
Access Roads
Waterways

Mount Whitney

TO LOS ANGELES

N
W   E
S

INTRODUCTION

The John Muir Trail is one of the most popular trails in the country, and may very well be the best hiking trail in the world. It runs 210 miles through the most spectacular part of the Sierra Nevada, North America's longest continuous mountain range, as it connects Yosemite Valley with Mount Whitney. On top of the great scenery, the Sierra boasts the best weather of any of the world's major mountain ranges. Bright sunny days are the rule, not the exception, which is what led John Muir to call the Sierra the "Range of Light." The trail itself is well marked, and well maintained. These factors are appreciated by hikers and packers who come from throughout the United States, Europe, and the rest of the world to see the sights along the trail.

In addition to being a path through world-class, awe-inspiring scenery, fishermen will be happy to learn that the John Muir Trail serves as a connection to many fine trout-fishing opportunities. As you follow the trail from Yosemite National Park in the north, through the Ansel Adams and John Muir Wilderness areas in the central Sierra, to Kings Canyon and Sequoia national parks in the south, plenty of wild trout are encountered. The trail passes 40 sparkling trout-filled lakes, crosses another 40 fish-inhabited creeks, and follows six of California's biggest, untamed freestone rivers in its journey along the crest of the Sierra. These waters are home to colorful and wild rainbow, brook, brown, and golden trout. The trout are so abundant that you can easily catch dozens per day if you know where to spend your fishing time. Although generally not huge, there are many places where you'll find fish of 12 to 14 inches and a few spots where even bigger trout live. I've seen 15-inch brook trout, 16-inch goldens, and 20-inch browns in the lakes and rivers along the trail.

If you are one who delights in being surrounded by alpine splendor while casting for trout in relative solitude, the John Muir Trail may be for you. If you enjoy fishing along rivers and creeks in their most natural states, above dams and parking lots, where people are scarce and wild trout are numerous (instead of the other way around), the John Muir Trail is probably for you. If you long for trout fishing in its purest form, in land preserved for perpetuity—fishing the way it was generations ago and is likely to remain, unchanged, for generations to come—the John Muir Trail is definitely for you.

The desire to seek unspoiled beauty grows each year as populations increase and our cities become more crowded. The rare valuable places that are forever protected from development, such as the high Sierra, will be even more treasured in the years to come.

In 1873, while John Muir was preparing to leave on his first trip down the entire high Sierra, from Yosemite to the top of Mt. Whitney, he said "The mountains are calling me, and I must go." So I say, more than a century later, if the mountain trout are calling you, and you must go, the high Sierra is an ideal place to answer that call, and the John Muir Trail will take you through the best it has to offer.

Little has changed in the high mountains in the 125 years since Muir spoke those words and set off on the trip he felt so strongly compelled to take. The biggest changes, fortunately for us, are that there are more trout up there now than there were in his day, and there is a nice trail to follow. What hasn't changed at all is the character of the mountains and the pure feel of the wilderness. So, like Muir on his trip, you'll likely find refreshment of body and soul as you cast your way along water so pristine, and hike through land so unspoiled and stunningly dramatic, that few people can even imagine it still exists in California at the threshold of the twenty-first century.

A large high-country rainbow rises to a dry fly. Surprisingly, rainbow are not the most common trout type found in waters along the trail.

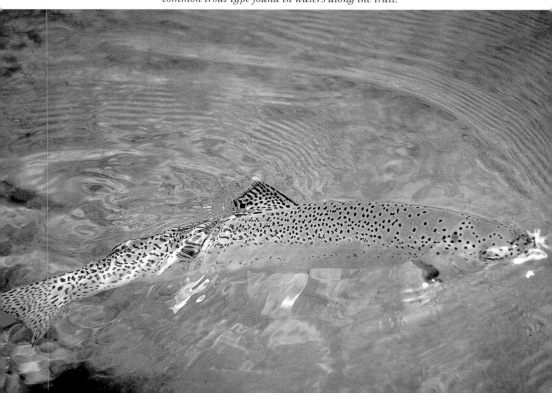

PREPARING
FOR YOUR TRIP TO THE JOHN MUIR TRAIL

This guide covers the trail from north to south, simply because that is the direction I traveled while hiking. I chose to start in the north because I live close to Yosemite Valley, the northern end point of the trail. The number of hikers who start in the north seems to be about the same as those who start at the southern end, at Mt. Whitney. Proponents of starting in the south cite the advantage of beginning their hike at a higher elevation (8500 feet at Whitney Portal vs. 4000 feet at Happy Isles in Yosemite Valley), so when the trail has been completed, they will have saved 4500 feet of climbing. Some hikers like to start in the north because early in the season the high southern passes may still be covered in deep snow, while the northern passes may be clear. Both starting points have their relative advantages, so there is no clear-cut answer to the question of which is the best end from which to start. The decision is determined as often by weather conditions as by individual preference, but the most important decision to be made is not the direction of travel, but the season of travel. This is especially true since the large majority of hikers do only a portion of the trail at a time, rather than tackle the whole thing at once.

Seasons
For fishing as well as hiking, the prime season to be on the trail is from July to September. In some years you can find good trail conditions and ice-free lakes in June, but that is usually only true at the lowest parts of the trail. A much more likely scenario would find the trail clear of snow and the weather warm enough to hike and fish during October. However, in a typical year, neither June or October can be counted on to provide co-operative weather conditions, so it is safest to plan your trip for July, August, or September. Each of those months has its advantages and its drawbacks in both the hiking and fishing departments. When planning far in advance, consider the following factors when picking a time to go:

July (early season): Positives: Less people on the trail, fearless trout that may not have seen fishermen for a year, good insect hatches, plenty of water in creeks—for trout habitat and for hikers to drink. Negatives: Rough weather possible, mosquitoes could be plentiful, rivers and creeks without bridges could be high and difficult, or at least time-consuming, to cross.

August (mid-season): Positives: Warm, dependable weather, easier creek fords, few mosquitoes. Negatives: Trout could be sluggish or timid, trail could be busy—this is the most popular time.

September (late season): Positives: Least number of people on trail, trout perking up with cooler temperatures, trout more concentrated in lower water—making them easier to locate, very few mosquitoes, easy creek crossings with less wet fords, weather usually still very good. Negatives: Few insect hatches, low water—making fish harder to approach and drinking water less plentiful, days getting shorter.

Fishing Regulations

There are no special fishing regulations in effect anywhere along the trail. The regular California trout limits and fishing seasons are also in effect in the national parks and wilderness areas. A California fishing license is required, but no special licenses or permits are needed.

Hiking and Camping Regulations

Wilderness permits are required for overnight stays on all areas of the trail. The permits are free if obtained in person at Forest Service or National Park offices. They can also be applied for through the mail for a $3.00 handling fee (per party, per trip). There are quotas limiting the number of hikers allowed on each trail, so the sooner you make your plans and apply for your permit the better. In general, about 1/2 of the permits for each trail are available for advance reservation. The reservations can be made from about 6 months to two days before departure. The remaining 1/2 are held for first-come, first-served hikers who pick them up in person on the day of departure, or one day before.

Wilderness Permits and General Information Addresses and Contact Numbers

YOSEMITE NATIONAL PARK

Wilderness Permits:
Yosemite National Park
Wilderness Permits
P.O. Box 545
Yosemite, CA 95389
(209) 372-0740

General Information:
Yosemite National Park
P.O. Box 577
Yosemite, CA 95389
(209) 372-0265
www.nps.gov/yose

SEQUOIA AND KINGS CANYON NATIONAL PARKS

Wilderness Permits
Sequoia & Kings Canyon
   National Parks
Wilderness Permit Reservations
Three Rivers, CA 93271
Fax (559) 565-3797

General Information:
Sequoia & Kings Canyon
   National Parks
Three Rivers, CA 93271
(559) 565-3341
www.nps.gov/seki

INYO NATIONAL FOREST

Wilderness Permits:
Inyo National Forest
Wilderness Reservation Service
P.O. Box 430
Big Pine, CA 93513
(888) 374-3773
Fax (760) 938-1137

General Information:
Inyo National Forest

White Mountain Ranger District
798 N. Main Street
Bishop, CA 93514
(760) 873-2500
Reservations for hiking the whole trail, starting in the south, contact:
Mt. Whitney Ranger Station
P.O. Box 8
Lone Pine, CA 93545
(760) 876-6200

Wilderness Permits and General Information:
Pineridge Ranger District
P.O. Box 559
Prather, CA 93651
(559) 855-5360
Sequoia National Forest

Wilderness Permits:
Supervisor's Office
900 W. Grand Avenue
Porterville, CA 93257
(559) 784-1500

General Information:
Sequoia National Forest
32588 Highway 190
Springville, CA 93265
(559) 539-2607

Some people complain about the necessity of obtaining a permit. Yes, it can be inconvenient, and certainly disappointing, if you find a trail has filled and you are unable to carry out your plans. Looking on the positive side though, at least the permit and quota systems assure that the backcountry won't be overcrowded. It may seem crowded at the most popular spots if every trailhead reaches its maximum limit, but any given area won't be over-run with hordes of hikers, which could happen if there were no limitations. With the permit system, it can only be crowded to a certain point.

During the peak season, in August of a typical year, I still only meet an average of one or two hikers an hour on the bulk of the trail (the exceptions are the places where roads touch the trail—at each end, and at Tuolumne Meadows and Devils Postpile—where more people are usually seen). I have hiked entire days on the trail without seeing anyone, but those times and places are rare during the summer months.

There are campfire restrictions in effect in the national parks. In Yosemite, no campfires are allowed above the 9600-foot elevation, in Kings Canyon the maximum is 10,000 feet, and in Sequoia the top elevation is 11,200 feet. The purpose of the restrictions is to protect the fragile timberline environment where trees are scarce and slow growing.

A few individual lakes and creek drainages are currently closed to camping. These are shown on maps and mentioned in guide books. The closures are subject to change, so the latest information is usually covered in detail when a wilderness permit is obtained for a certain area.

Hiking Guides

There are two hiking guides that cover the entire trail thoroughly and have proven their worth over time. I feel comfortable recommending either and I've used them both. The first, *Starr's Guide to the John Muir Trail* by Walter Starr Jr., is the classic and long-time favorite that has been in print since 1934. It is still accurate and useful. The modern-day standard is *The John Muir Trail* by Thomas Winnett, which was first published in 1978, and has been updated and revised many times since then. Winnett's book has the advantage of being more recent, so some of the subtle changes in the trail are covered. When I hiked the trail for the first time I read each before I went, and I also carried them both with me. It isn't necessary to pack them both—

you wouldn't go wrong with either one—I just brought them along for reading material as I spent weeks alone on the trail.

Maps

There are three sources for accurate and detailed topographic hiking maps. The trail is well signed and easy to follow, but even after hiking it several times I wouldn't consider doing it without good maps. I refer to them often as I hike, to check my progress, plan my stops for fishing and camping, and identify landmarks.

The U.S. Geological Survey publishes the topographic maps that have been used for generations. These are currently only being produced in a small scale (7.5 minute series), so they aren't very convenient to use. If you are going to stay on the trail, these maps give you more detail than you need, requiring a long-range hiker to carry an excessive number of them to cover the trail. They are most useful (often indispensable) for cross-country travel because of their great detail.

The Wilderness Press publishes maps that cover the entire trail on a larger, more convenient scale (15 minute series). These have other advantages over the U.S.G.S. maps in that they are more up-to-date and also more durable (waterproof and more resistant to tearing).

A relatively new and convenient map set for hikers doing the entire trail is the "John Muir Trail Map Pack" published by Tom Harrison Cartography. This set of 13 maps is on the same scale as the 15 minute series, but is printed on small (8 1/2 x 11) sheets that are extremely easy to use while hiking. You put away the 12 maps you won't need for the day, leaving a nice small page that you can keep in a shirt pocket and unfold quickly and easily even in a heavy wind without having it turn into a sail. These maps zero in on the trail, so you don't have to carry a lot of extra paper that you don't need. An additional handy feature is that the trail mileage between points is printed on the maps.

You can get these maps at sporting goods stores, ranger stations, and the Visitor Centers in the national parks. They can also be ordered by mail or telephone by directly contacting the publishers:

U.S. Geological Survey
345 Middlefield Road
Menlo Park, CA 94025
1-(888) 275-8747 Fax: (650) 329-5130
www.usgs.gov

Wilderness Press
2440 Bancroft Way
Berkeley, CA 94704
1-(800) 443-7227

Tom Harrison Cartography
2 Falmouth Cove
San Rafael, CA 94901
1-(800) 265-9090

John Muir was once asked what he did in preparation for a hiking trip to the mountains, he answered, "step over the back fence."
**If you're ready to step over your fence,
let's go fish the John Muir Trail!**

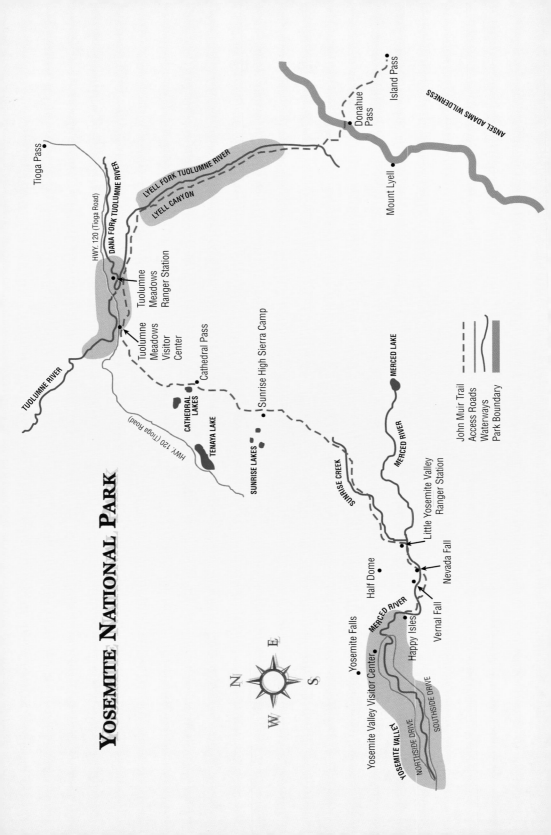

Fishing Along the Trail

YOSEMITE NATIONAL PARK

While driving up Highway 395, heading home after a week-long solo hiking trip in the southern Sierra, I was caught off guard by my emotions. I had just been through some unbelievably beautiful mountains—country that I'd never seen before, but instead of reveling in the memories of that experience, I found myself growing increasingly charged up as I neared Yosemite. I was getting closer to my family and my home, which had to be part of my eagerness, and although Yosemite has seemed like my second home in recent years, I still was surprised by the warmth and nostalgia I felt as I reached the entrance at Tioga Pass.

The park does have a certain magnetism that, I guess, can never be lost. Certainly John Muir never lost his affection for Yosemite even after he spent a lifetime exploring the entire Sierra and mountain ranges throughout the world. As the last light was fading, leaving a trace of alpenglow on the mountains, I drove into Tuolumne Meadows. I absolutely got chills down my spine as I gazed at the scene I'd seen a hundred times before. I feel the same emotions each spring when I enter Yosemite Valley and see the new life springing forth. The waterfalls are awakening from their dormancy, filling the valley with sound and the Merced River with energy. The river flows through

The Merced River, Vernal Fall, Nevada Fall, and Half Dome. "... As if into this one mountain mansion Nature had gathered her choicest treasures." — John Muir

the newly lush green meadows as the bright sunshine lights the granite walls. Insects are hatching, and the trout are beginning to stir. Familiarity, where Yosemite is concerned, has bred comfort and abiding love.

The National Park Service began cutting back on fish planting in Yosemite during the 1970s, and eliminated the practice completely in 1991. Today, all

At the start of the trail, Happy Isles in Yosemite Valley.

the trout in Yosemite are wild fish. The Yosemite section of the trail gets as much use as any other stretch, and it stacks up well against the rest of the trail in both the scenery and fishing departments.

The First Steps

You don't ease into the John Muir Trail (JMT) from either direction. Whether you start from Yosemite Valley or from Whitney Portal, you begin hiking uphill immediately. You're also likely to have plenty of company at both ends of the trail. If you start from Yosemite Valley, the first 8 miles will be the lowest in elevation of your entire trip. Don't be fooled into thinking that you brought too much warm clothing—chances are you'll need it sometime in the next 200 miles. The elevation at the trail's start, Happy Isles in Yosemite Valley, is 4035 feet. After those first few miles, never again will the trail dip below 7400 feet, and only rarely will it be below 8000 feet. For most of the trail, the elevation ranges from 9000 to 11,000 feet.

Merced River

Right from the start, it's worth noting that, in general, the higher the elevation, the shorter the growing season for the trout. This is important to

The northern end of the trail, the Merced River in Yosemite Valley. "No temple made with hands can compare with Yosemite" — John Muir

BETH BECK PHOTO

remember when starting in Yosemite so that you don't overlook the fine fishing in the Merced River as you charge out of the gate on your way to what might be the adventure of a lifetime. The natural tendency, especially for through-hikers, (those doing the entire trail

in one trip), is to keep the rod packed away on the first day. All the planning, excitement, and anticipation that have led up to actually strapping on the pack at the trailhead can cause even dedicated anglers to forget about everything except getting on down the trail. It's very difficult to stop and fish halfway through the first day, when energy and adrenaline are at their peaks. Actually, it's not any easier for the northbound through hiker to pause and enjoy the fishing when the oft dreamed of finish line is only minutes away—and downhill at that.

Even the fact that some of the largest trout on the trail can be found in

Author fishing the Merced River below Half Dome.

the Merced River won't be enough to persuade the majority of anglers to give it a try. Many also bypass the Merced because they don't think it could possibly hold any decent fish. Because of all the people they see hiking the trail above the river, they assume that all the good fish have been caught.

Releasing a 3-pound brown trout taken from the Merced River near the start of the trail in Yosemite.

From Yosemite Valley upstream to Nevada Fall is without a doubt the most heavily traveled section of the JMT. There are, however, some nice wild brown and rainbow trout in this section that, surprisingly, sees few fishermen during an average summer day. This is a rugged, boulder-strewn stretch of water that makes for rough going—no doubt discouraging many potential fishermen. Hundreds of people hike the trail every day on their way to see world-famous Vernal and Nevada falls. In the scores of times that I've been fortunate enough to take this hike, I've probably seen less than 10 people fishing the river. The pockets and plunge pools hold equal numbers of browns and rainbows that are usually in the 8- to 12-inch range. The browns will be slightly bigger on average; I've taken them up to 15 inches. I've also caught some pretty 13-inch rainbows from the best holes in this, one of my favorite rivers.

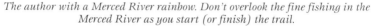

The author with a Merced River rainbow. Don't overlook the fine fishing in the Merced River as you start (or finish) the trail.

Before leaping over Nevada Fall, one of the most spectacular waterfalls in Yosemite, (a statement that automatically qualifies it as one of the most spectacular in the world) the Merced runs placidly through scenic Little Yosemite Valley. The level trail follows the smoothly flowing river for about a mile, affording the fisherman a good opportunity to be seduced by easily visible brown trout dimpling the surface. A large percentage of hikers make this their initial night's camp, breaking out their fishing rods for the first of many times. This is a good idea, for the Little Yosemite Valley run of the Merced is home to a healthy population of browns that average 10 inches, and a lesser number of rainbows that are slightly smaller.

The trout can be difficult to approach in this smooth, crystal-clear water, so fishing at times of low light will yield better results, as will using long, light leaders with small flies. Occasionally, exceptional browns are spotted here—fish in the 14- to 18-inch class—but its rare that these big wary fish are hooked. A foot-long brown is a fine catch in Little Yosemite, and usually it will take a good effort from a crafty angler to land one. This is classic dry-fly, brown-trout water—a fine place to start a fishing journey along the JMT.

Near the campsites, the trail leaves Little Yosemite Valley and climbs along Sunrise Creek. The lower section of the creek is virtually fishless, but where the trail nears the creek, close to the Clouds Rest Trail, small rainbows become common. For the next several miles as the trail climbs toward Sunrise High Sierra Camp, pleasant little Sunrise Creek is never far away. The promising holes all hold their share of 5- to 9-inch rainbows, as the trout are plentiful in this middle stretch.

Some of the trout in the middle part of the creek look more like cutthroat than rainbow. Further upstream, above a series of cascades, the rainbow characteristics disappear, and the trout seem to be pure cutthroats. I've been unable to find any record of an official planting of cutts in the creek, but the markings are unmistakable. These fish aren't any bigger or any more

Nevada Fall of the Merced River. John Muir's favorite, it's one of the most impressive waterfalls in Yosemite, the Sierra, and the world.

The Merced River flows peacefully through Little Yosemite Valley, a popular camping spot.

colorful than their downstream rainbow cousins, but they do hold some novelty value for the angler. This is the only place on the JMT where cutthroat are encountered, so if you want to catch all five varieties of trout, be sure to take a few minutes to stalk the banks of upper Sunrise Creek. Tactics on this, as on most small creeks, call for short casts with dry flies following a stealthy approach from downstream. Please release all you catch, so the next person will have the unique experience of catching a cutthroat trout in California.

A spectacular side trip to the top of Half Dome is highly recommended for hikers who find themselves with extra time and energy. There are no fish en route, but the experience of climbing the cables and the subsequent view from the top is well worthwhile. The same can be said for the side trip to Clouds Rest, which sports a view on par with any in Yosemite, the Sierra, and perhaps the world.

If a fishing side trip is desired, a short hike off the JMT to the Sunrise

Small but unique. A short stretch of Sunrise Creek is the only place on the trail where cutthroat trout are found.

Trout Fishing the JOHN MUIR TRAIL

Lakes would be a good choice. Just a mile over the hill from the Sunrise Camp, the lakes hold nice brook trout. Upper Sunrise, the first lake encountered, has brookies up to, and sometimes exceeding, the one-foot mark.

In the highly scenic Sunrise Camp area, the trail follows a fishless creek through Long Meadow as it heads for Cathedral Pass—the first and lowest of the 10 passes on the trail. On the other side of the pass, you quickly drop to Upper Cathedral Lake, which sits at the foot of distinctive Cathedral Peak. This is a popular campsite, just as most lakes that sit near passes tend to be. This is the case because hikers heading down from a pass are usually ready for a rest,

Cathedral Range from Sunrise Camp.
The awesome alpine scenery is virtually non-stop on the entire trail.

and often camp at the first decent spot that has water. Likewise, hikers approaching a pass may wish to rest before going over, and also frequently end up camping at the lake closest to the pass. In the case of Upper Cathedral Lake, it has even more visitors because it's a popular spot for day hikers who come from Tuolumne Meadows. This combination has had an impact on the trout population in the lake, but the impact hasn't been all negative.

Over the years, Cathedral has been heavily fished, and now has only a small population of brook trout. The brookies average about 9 inches, but since some are harvested, they don't overpopulate and end up stunting each other's growth. Because their numbers are low, the competition among them for the available food is also low, which allows a few to grow old and large.

One memorable day in September of 1996 I was fortunate enough to catch a beautiful brook trout of 14 inches in Upper Cathedral. It made my day, but was the only fish I caught in the lake that afternoon.

The next few miles past Cathedral Lake are downhill toward the justly popular, beautiful Tuolumne Meadows. With the meadows in view, you cross little Budd Creek with its surprisingly nice-sized brook trout. I've caught 9- and 10-inch brookies that looked like sharks in this tiny creek. The creek isn't densely populated with trout, which explains their good average size.

Tuolumne River

As the trail breaks out of the trees into gorgeous and spacious Tuolumne Meadows, hikers soon understand why solitude is a rarity on this stretch of trail. I consider Tuolumne Meadows to be one of the most pleasantly beautiful places in the Sierra. The five-mile-long meadow is surrounded by distinctive snow-capped peaks, with the Tuolumne River running right through the middle of the peaceful splendor. Since a road (Highway 120) provides immediate access, there are always plenty of people delighting in the scenery. Fishermen needn't worry about crowds on the water though. Surprisingly, despite being one of the most popular hiking and camping destinations in the

Wading the Tuolumne River in spacious Tuolumne Meadows. "In every way the most delightful summer pleasure-park in all the High Sierra." — John Muir

BETH BECK PHOTO

Sierra, the Tuolumne River in the meadows doesn't get heavily fished. One possible explanation for the lack of fishing pressure might be the small average size of the trout. There are ample quantities of brown trout in the 8- to 10-inch range, as well as a small population of brook trout. There are enough 10- to 12-inch browns to keep things interesting for advanced anglers, but fish over a foot long are few and far between.

What probably discourages some fishermen is not a lack of trout, or lack of trout size, but rather the difficulty they have in catching them. The crystal-clear river meanders slowly through the grassy meadow, creating conditions that magnify the casting mistakes and careless approaches that quickly send the trout into hiding. It isn't an easy place to catch fish, even if there are plenty to be had, but fly-casters have an advantage over spin-fishers when trying for these wary browns.

I've found the best flies to be terrestrial patterns fished near the bank, with small black ant patterns being the prime choice all summer long. Early in the summer a large flying ant hatches in the area, and the trout seem to key into it. The ant can be matched by using a size 12 Sierra Bug (a black fly with a white wing). Later in the summer, smaller terrestrial ants are common. Most are found around people's picnic lunches, but many also end up as lunch for the trout. Trout relish ants, and Tuolumne Meadows trout are no exception.

I've caught few trout over 12 inches in the meadow and have only seen one bigger than 14 inches—but it was a lot bigger. Over the years I'd heard stories about monster browns in Tuolumne Meadows, but like most "big brown trout" stories, there wasn't anything concrete—just rumor and sec- ond- or third-hand hearsay. I'd fished there enough to discount such stories as exaggerated, or at least outdated. My mind was changed one day in the fall of 1987 when I had a first-hand experience. I was sneaking upstream prepar- ing to cast for a typical 10-inch brown that was rising tight to the bank, when a big dark shape caught my eye. The shape that had materialized from the river bottom swam toward me, momentarily became a huge brown trout, then disappeared under the bank I was standing on. I had a good look at it, and after convincing myself that it wasn't a mirage, I estimated it to be a trout about two feet long! I stayed around for awhile, making numerous casts, but I never saw it again. Now I can be added to the list of people who claim to have seen one of the Tuolumne Meadows monster browns.

At the campfire that evening, my wife and I joked about big-fish sightings being similar to UFO sightings. She had been upstream reading a book and hadn't seen the fish, which is typical—these things usually happen when you're alone with no witnesses to corroborate your story. I still haven't talked to anyone who's actually caught one of these mammoths, but at least I now know for sure that they exist, and I feel fortunate just to have seen one.

Another terrestrial pattern that yields good results is the grasshopper. On warm, breezy summer days, the kind of lazy days when you'd least expect the fishing to be good, the hoppers in the meadows become active. Some get blown into the river where hungry trout are waiting to pounce on them like Mark McGwire going after a hanging curve ball. Tan and yellow patterns in sizes 10-12 will imitate most of the hoppers found in the area. If a fly fisher- man catches one of the rare, outsized browns from Tuolumne Meadows, I think a hopper will be the fly that does the job.

The main Tuolumne River is formed when its two primary forks, the Lyell and Dana forks, join in Tuolumne Meadows. Soon after leaving the meadow, the JMT crosses each fork, starting with the fast-moving Dana Fork. The stretch near the JMT is pocket water containing small holes that aren't big enough to qualify as pools. The Dana Fork carries less water than the Lyell Fork, but is more densely populated with trout. This shallow, fast water is a delight to fish with dry flies, although the fish won't break a lot of leaders. Brown, brook, and rainbow trout are all found in the 6- to 10-inch range. Browns predominate, and are generally slightly larger as well.

Less than a half mile after leaving the swift Dana Fork, the trail crosses the

The Lyell Fork of the Tuolumne River near the bridge crossing. "No finer fishing can be found in the world than is had in this stream..." — Yosemite Park Superintendent, 1905.

other main fork, the Lyell Fork, on a sturdy bridge through another beautiful meadow. Here, the hiker gets a taste of what's to come for the next 9 miles through Lyell Canyon. The trail follows the peaceful river through grassy meadows, affording unlimited opportunities to cast dry flies to rising trout. It can be difficult to make good hiking time on these easy level trail miles if you're a dry-fly enthusiast. The trail is seldom far from the river, and off-trail travel is easy along the banks, so fishing breaks are justifiably frequent.

The Lyell Canyon is a gorgeous place in a peaceful, unspectacular way. The clear water running gently through the meadows, surrounded by snow-capped peaks, can be mesmerizing. Throw in a healthy population of wild trout, and it can be anticipated that non-fishing members of a hiking party will find themselves with plenty of time to observe the beauty while waiting for the fishermen.

The Lyell Fork has long been held in high regard for its quality fishing. In 1905, the acting superintendent of Yosemite wrote the following in his annual report to the US Secretary of the Interior: "No finer fishing can be found in the world than is had in this stream, nine miles in length, which runs through a continuous meadow and whose banks are clear of all growth. The depth of the stream varies from two to six feet, with many pools twenty feet in depth." Little has changed in the past century.

The lower miles hold brook, brown, and rainbow trout, generally in the 6- to 10-inch range, with a few reaching 12 inches (as usual, the bigger fish are browns). This was one of the first waters planted in Yosemite. Brook trout were introduced in 1878 by early settlers, before Yosemite was a national park (actually, this was before there was any such thing as a national park

Trout Fishing the JOHN MUIR TRAIL

This photogenic lake is no secret to fishing and non-fishing backpackers alike. On a four-day, early July trip from Tuolumne Meadows to Devils Postpile, I counted ten other fishermen—nine of them at Thousand Island Lake. In addition, there were another half dozen non-fishermen at the lake. The fishermen were concentrated near the outlet by the trail crossing. Not only did this turn out to be the most fishermen I've seen at any lake on the JMT, but they were all within a few hundred yards of each other on a lake that's two miles long. They weren't, it turns out, all clumped together just for the sake of convenience; most were catching some of the lake's brook and rainbow trout. The area in and around the outlet creek has a better concentration of fish than the rest of the lake.

I saw very few trout on a long walk along the lake's far shore, and was a bit disappointed in the average size of the trout in this huge lake. The brook trout, planted in the 1940s, run up to only about 9 inches. The slightly bigger rainbow trout were planted first in 1930, many times in the following years, and have been planted annually in the 1990s. Unfortunately the rainbows rarely exceed 10 inches.

Reproduction is considered good for both rainbow and brook, but the DFG still feels the need to plant rainbow fingerlings to supplement the naturally reproducing trout due to heavy fishing pressure and the harvesting that goes with it. Some interesting fish plants were attempted in the 1930s when both steelhead and cutthroat trout were planted, but neither survived.

Anyone willing to make the long walk to the inlet side of the lake would be rewarded with solitude as well as some of the lake's better rainbows. Grasshoppers are a good fly choice in this and in many high-country lakes during mid-summer. The scenery at Thousand Island is enough reason to visit, but the lake also provides lively trout-fishing in some parts.

The outlet creek is also an enjoyable place for fly fishermen to pick up some good rainbows. Nymphing the fast water and casting dry caddis patterns in the pockets turned up a couple of feisty 10- to 12-inch rainbows for me.

The outlet creek is the main headwater source for the Middle Fork of the San Joaquin River. You could leave the JMT here, follow the Upper San Joaquin via trails for a few miles, and rejoin the JMT at points south. Strictly from a fishing standpoint, such a detour makes sense, as the fishing is good on the San Joaquin.

Leaving the crowds at Thousand Island Lake, you quickly come to Emerald Lake, where there is generally only a small population of rainbows. They've been planted in every decade since the 1930s, and don't seem able to successfully reproduce. Currently planted annually, the fishing is entirely dependent on the stocking allocations and growth of the hatchery fingerlings. At times, the trout grow well in Emerald, reaching 12 to 14 inches with some regularity. In 1997 I saw only a dozen or so, mostly in the 8- to 10-inch range. For numbers of trout, the lake has never been a great producer, but for size, it has shown the ability to grow big fish. If you time it correctly and search hard for pods of fish, you can take some nice rainbows at pleasant Emerald Lake.

Close by, another small lake, Ruby, is also planted annually with rainbows. Unlike Emerald, Ruby has reproduction capacity, so wild rainbows turn up from time to time. The majority of fish, however, will be hatchery transplants in the 6- to 9-inch range. Rarely, a rainbow will reach 12 or 13 inches, but most will be small with little coloration. All the trout I caught at Ruby were very pale—silver and black instead of the red and green you usually find on wild rainbows. Because of their color (or lack thereof) we started calling them

"Oakland Raider" trout. First planted in 1940, the lake was found to be self-sustaining, so it wasn't planted again until 1959. Ruby doesn't get much fishing pressure, so there are usually plenty of trout to go around.

Garnet Lake

The next lake to the south is huge Garnet Lake. Garnet could fool you into thinking you'd made a wrong turn and gone in a circle back to Thousand Island Lake. It is of similar size and shape to Thousand Island, and also is poised at the base of the marvelous pair of mountains, Ritter and Banner. Counting the islands would give it away, but counting the fish probably wouldn't. Like Thousand Island, Garnet is home to rainbow and brook trout, and was also planted with cutthroat and steelhead (which are no longer found here, either). Spawning conditions are generally poor, but spawning is possible in some years. The rainbows have been known to reach 14 inches, and the brook trout about 13 inches, but most are under 10.

The outlet creek below the fall holds a fairly dense population of brookies immediately below the lake. Once they leave for Garnet Creek, the trout can't return to the lake due to the waterfall. Years ago there was some concern about big spawners leaving the lake and not returning. As a result, in 1941 a fish barrier screen was installed at the lake's outlet. The barrier has been removed, so Garnet Creek once again holds mature fish that have left the lake, in addition to its streamborn residents.

Garnet has a fairly sparse population of trout, and like Thousand Island (more similarities), depends on planting to maintain its numbers. Spawning is possible but very limited for rainbow, so Garnet has been planted almost annually since 1930 with large quantities of rainbow fingerlings. Excellent fishing has been reported at times, but being dependent on planting, fishing conditions can change regularly.

Like its twin (Thousand Island), I'd rate the fishing in Garnet as only fair. Although not as visually spectacular as Thousand Island (that's an extremely tough comparison since I consider Thousand Island to be one of the most scenic lakes in all the Sierra), Garnet is located in an outstanding setting.

After climbing out of the Garnet Lake Basin, the trail reaches the edge of a spacious meadow where full-flowing Shadow Creek teems with stunted brook trout. The trout are scarce downstream of the meadow where this lovely creek cascades toward Shadow Lake.

Another of the area's scenic jewels, Shadow Lake's reputation for beauty, and its close proximity to trailheads, has led to overuse. It is currently closed to camping, which may help improve the fishing in future years. Located four miles from the road at Agnew Meadows, many day-hikers visit and fish Shadow Lake—making it, over the years, among the most heavily fished lakes in the area.

Shadow was planted with several types of trout, starting with goldens in the 1930s and 40s. The goldens were unable to reproduce and haven't been seen since 1953. Brook trout were planted from 1948-1951, and even those hardy fish have had a tough time surviving at the heavily fished lake. Rainbows have been planted regularly since 1950, and have been on an annual schedule in the 1990s. The small number of brook trout that have been able to survive and reproduce have never attained much size. The same is true of the rainbow fingerlings, which also rarely have grown bigger than 10 inches.

Through the years that records have been kept, the DFG reports that fishing has always been regarded as poor by anglers visiting Shadow Lake. There have never been a lot of fish caught, and the ones caught were usually small. A small population of small trout—not exactly the combination that draws fishermen to a lake. With a recent poor reputation for fishing, and a camping closure now in effect, perhaps fishing prospects for the planted rainbows will show some improvement in the coming years at this pleasant lake. On my last visit I didn't see any other fishermen, but the bad news is I didn't see any adult fish either—just the recently planted fingerlings.

After climbing steeply away from the eye-pleasing Shadow Lake, you arrive at the wooded shores of Rosalie Lake, another rainbow trout lake that relies on annual plants to maintain its population. It was first planted in 1932, but the fish have never been able to reproduce consistently. Reproduction is thought to be possible in very wet years only, but the fingerlings do fairly well in the lake—some have reached 16 inches in past years. I found large quantities of 5- to 10-inch rainbows well distributed throughout the lake. These fish were pale in color, like the Ruby Lake rainbows.

The outlet creek also supports healthy numbers of trout in similar sizes to those found in the lake. I did take one rainbow in the creek that had some fine markings and the nice coloration of a wild trout—evidence that some natural reproduction is taking place. The outlet creek descends gently for only about a hundred yards before plunging down a cliff to join the San Joaquin River. I wouldn't count on spending much fishing time at Rosalie, but if you find yourself camping there, it does provide fair sport.

Upon leaving the solid but unspectacular fishing at Rosalie Lake, a fisherman wouldn't miss any memorable angling by packing away the rod for awhile. In the next several miles the trail passes a number of small lakes and lakelets that are fishless, or nearly so. First, pretty little Gladys Lake is skirted, with its meager population of little rainbows. It's planted every year, so there are a few catchable fish present when water conditions are favorable for consecutive years.

The next lake south of Gladys is another small, shallow lake with a woman's name. Vivian Lake is unnamed on most maps, so it is difficult to determine exactly which lake it is. The DFG apparently had trouble differentiating between Vivian and Gladys, as their stocking records are mixed up and overlap between the two (maybe the lakes were named for identical twins). Anyway, it doesn't much matter about the mix-up, because the two lakes are similar from a fishing standpoint. Vivian also has a limited population of rainbows, and also has poor reproduction capabilities since it too is shallow and subject to winterkill. The end result is that neither lake is worthy of the angler's attention. Unfortunately, the same can be said of the next few lakes encountered, the Trinity Lakes and Johnston Lake. None of these are planted anymore, due to the poor survival record of the past plants.

The string of poor fishing in the lakes of the last several miles may result in disappointment for anglers. Consolation and an uplift in spirits may be found when reaching the cool, clear-flowing waters of delightful Minaret Creek. An average-sized creek with a good flow, it's loaded with frisky, colorful brook, rainbow, and rainbow/golden hybrid trout. Brookies in the 6- to 9-inch range are the most common catch, while rainbows and hybrids up to 11 inches are sometimes encountered. The creek was planted with rainbows many times starting in 1930, and with brook trout once, very successfully, in 1947.

Just downstream from the JMT, Minaret Creek becomes multi-branched as it cascades over Minaret Falls, a pleasant sight in the early season. This attractive creek is an ideal place to drift dry flies for an hour, an afternoon, or a day.

It's so enjoyable to fish Minaret Creek that it contributed to Rod and I missing the last shuttle bus from Devils Postpile up to Mammoth. We were on a four-day trip with only one deadline to meet: Thursday's 6:30 shuttle bus to Mammoth—where our wives would be waiting (and waiting some more as it turns out). Beth and Rena weren't too pleased when we didn't get off the final bus of the day. Luckily we had a better excuse than "Minaret Creek was too much fun—the fish were rising everywhere and we lost track of time." I'll admit, we did spend more time at the creek than planned, but we still thought we'd left in plenty of time to make the bus. The real problem was that when we reached the Middle Fork of the San Joaquin River at Devils Postpile, the bridge was out—a casualty of the massive 1997 winter floods. We were able to easily wade across the river at a spot that we picked out quickly. The big river seemed tame compared to the Rush Creek crossing of two days earlier. Tame or not, the wet crossing still caused us to lose valuable minutes while we changed shoes. We got to the shuttle stop at 6:34, just in time to see the bus pulling away. Part of the blame certainly goes to the trout of Minaret Creek, but most of it must be shouldered by the San Joaquin River for knocking out the bridge—leaving Rod and I totally innocent of blame.

Middle Fork of the San Joaquin River

The trail parallels and crosses the Middle San Joaquin inside the boundaries of Devils Postpile National Monument. This region is extremely popular with campers and day hikers who stroll its network of trails. Fishermen are not an uncommon sight along the river, but they are relatively few and usually dispersed throughout a wide area, so you seldom feel crowded when working the water. On the trails however, you will usually feel crowded—especially after hiking the sparsely populated roadless sections of the JMT.

This part of the San Joaquin is a wading dry-fly fisherman's delight. Generally shallow, its riffles, pockets, and runs support a healthy population of 6- to 12-inch browns that are willing risers to dry flies all summer. I've found the best flies for mid-summer to be dries in sizes 12-16. Tan Elk Hair Caddis patterns do well to match the steady and prolific hatches of naturals on most summer days.

Catchable-sized rainbows are planted near the campgrounds where they entertain bait fishermen, and occasionally survive long enough to learn about natural food and extend their lives. Larger holdover rainbows are intermittently taken. Rainbow fingerlings have been planted consistently for over 50 years all along the river, from the Postpile vicinity upstream to Garnet Creek. The upstream stretch features colorful hybrids but downstream next to the JMT, the brown trout is king.

If you can pull yourself away from fishing this enjoyable river, or if your fishing takes you downstream away from the JMT, be sure to pause and treat yourself to the sight of Rainbow Falls. The slight detour that's required pays scenic dividends as you get an exceptional, close-up look at one of the most impressive waterfalls in the Sierra. The Middle San Joaquin offers excellent scenery and surprisingly good fishing—more than compensating for this overused section of the trail.

JOHN MUIR WILDERNESS, NORTH

··

Leaving the crowds behind, you exit the National Monument and quickly find solitude in the tall trees and tiny creeks to the south. The first of these, Boundary Creek, is just a fishless trickle, as are the spring-fed northern branches of Crater Creek.

This stretch of trail provides impressive views into the basin of the Middle San Joaquin, but no fishing opportunities exist until the main branch of Crater Creek is reached near Crater Meadow, which was planted many times in the 1930s with both cutthroat and rainbow trout. Subsequent plants of rainbows were made, and they are the surviving species. There is an excellent population of 6- to 11-inch rainbows in Crater Meadow, but they don't extend to Upper Crater Meadow. These colorful trout are classified as hybrids, showing their golden trout ancestry on their bright yellow sides. This is a fun little creek that may pleasantly surprise you when you see a trout larger than expected in the clear shallow water. The bigger fish take up residence in the tough-to-reach brushy runs.

Walking a few nearly level miles past Crater Creek takes you to another enjoyable, underappreciated, trout-filled spot, Deer Creek. Ignore the fishless north branch and concentrate on the main south branch that abounds with 6- to 10-inch hybrids. I found these fish to be as hungry for my flies as the mosquitoes were for me. The brushy creek at the trail crossing opens up in a pretty meadow about a hundred yards upstream; a place that I'd highly recommend to anyone wishing to spend more than a few minutes fishing the creek. Don't expect anything huge, but for a creek of relatively small size, it holds respectably sized trout. Using 5X tippet, I left flies in a couple of fish that struck hard. I figured those trout had to be at least 10 inches to pull that off (pun intended).

Deer Creek is a super place to fish during a hiking break. A word of warning though—you may stay longer than planned. On my last trip I decided to fish my way upstream for a half hour. While stringing up the rod, I found myself immediately being swarmed by mosquitoes. Doubting I'd stay for the full half hour under those conditions, I applied repellent and put on my head net before setting off upstream. An hour and a dozen trout later, I was back to the trail crossing and ready to try the downstream portion of the creek. Sometimes good fishing takes precedence over comfort (maybe I should amend that to say, oftentimes good fishing takes precedence over comfort—my wife thinks the latter would be more accurate in my case. For many anglers I think it's safe to add that great fishing usually takes precedence over comfort).

Once across Deer Creek, the trail follows a ridge high above Fish Valley, eventually meeting the Duck Pass Trail to Mammoth Lakes. Just a mile up this trail is immense Duck Lake, one of the deepest lakes in the Sierra. Historically this has been a very popular camping spot for JMT hikers—even though it's off the trail—but it is currently closed to camping. Not many through-hikers visit it anymore because of the closure, but if it ever re-opens to camping it will undoubtedly regain its popularity.

If you make the side trip to Duck Lake, you'll find an ample number of trout. For many years rainbows have been planted nearly every year in large quantities in an attempt to keep up with the pressure from the steady flow of fishermen that come in from Mammoth. First introduced in 1942, the rainbows reach 12 to 14 inches, with an average size of about 10 inches. Goldens were planted in the lake from 1930-1938, but their numbers have steadily declined and they are no longer present. The goldens were known to grow quickly, but had the habit of leaving the lake once they reached maturity. A fish barrier was installed at the outlet creek in the 1940s as an attempt to halt this migration. It fulfilled its purpose in keeping the mature fish in the lake, but only when it was being regularly maintained. The barrier was washed out and wasn't replaced, so consequently the goldens have given way to rainbows.

There is limited spawning potential for rainbows in the inlet stream, but not enough to overpopulate this 258-acre lake. The good numbers of fish are well distributed around the lake, helped by the annual rainbow plants and by the naturally reproducing brook trout. The brookies are numerous but smaller than the rainbows.

How plentiful are the trout in Duck Lake? To answer that question, I'll describe my first few casts on my last visit. As happens from time to time, the top section of my rod came off during a cast. It slid down the line until it was stopped by the fly. As I was reeling it in, hoping the fly would hold, I noticed a couple of trout following the section of rod. They followed all the way to my feet, only leaving when I pulled the piece of rod out of the water. If they'd struck at the rod tip where the fly was, there is a slight chance one of them could have been hooked. That would have lead to an unusual fish story. If another angler happened by and inquired about the fishing, I imagine a conversation along these lines:

> Any luck? Yep, I just caught a rainbow.
> What'd you get it on? A 9-foot, 5-weight Sage.
> No, you don't understand, not what rod, what lure?
> No, you don't understand, the rod was the lure.
> Yeah, right...whatever...have a good day buddy.

Although scenic, the fishing in Duck Lake doesn't strike me as outstanding enough to justify a side trip. But, if you're passing by, or camping there, it certainly is worth a few casts, as it does hold decent trout in its depths.

Purple Lake

Purple Lake sits right on the JMT, and is popular with sightseers and fishermen. This pleasant average-sized lake has been considered overcrowded for many years. It could be worse now that Duck Lake is closed to camping, but Purple is far enough from trailheads that it doesn't receive day-hiking visitors.

The lake holds enough trout to keep anglers entertained all season. The trout are beautiful hybrids ranging from 7 to 12 inches, and are spread throughout the lake. Rainbows were first planted in the 1930s, and are currently planted annually. I can't find any record of goldens being planted, in fact the only recorded plant besides rainbow are the steelhead plants of the late 1930s. Some of the trout I've caught looked like pure goldens, some looked like pure rainbows, while most were obviously hybrids of the two.

The natural reproduction is pretty good, but annual plants are made to sustain the population under heavy fishing pressure. Planting doesn't seem necessary, as I found the lake teeming with trout on my last visit (1997). If the planting is curtailed, perhaps the average size of the trout would increase while still leaving satisfactory quantities.

I approached the lake with apprehension because a fisherman I met on the trail gave me the impression it might be fishless. I didn't think this was likely, based on the up-to-date information I had from the DFG, and the outdated information I had in my fishing log. My brother Bill and I fished Purple in 1981 and had excellent results. My records show that we each took 10 trout in a full day's fishing—many of them 12 to 13 inches. At the time, that ranked as the best day of trout fishing either of us had ever experienced.

I had fond memories of the lake, which made the news I received on the trail even more disturbing. In 1981, I wasn't paying attention to the lake's spawning potential, I was just having fun catching trout. Then, 16 years later, hoping for a repeat of the fine fishing, I neared the lake and came across this guy who said, in response to my question about his fishing experiences, "I only know about Purple Lake. Don't go there." He didn't actually say it was fishless—look closely at his words. Fortunately, I've learned not to rely on trail talk for reliable fishing information. Usually you can find kernels of truth veiled in double talk if you learn to read between the lines. So, I wasn't worried, but I was concerned. Could the lake have gone downhill since the great fishing of 1981? Possibly. Could the DFG have erroneous information in its files which states that Purple has good natural reproduction and a high trout population? Not likely. As I rounded the last bend and descended to the lake, these questions were echoing through my mind. Haunting visions of a barren Purple Lake were played against pleasant memories of brothers, on semester break from college, netting colorful foot-long trout on a warm, carefree summer evening nearly two decades before. The truth was soon revealed. To my delight, my first gaze upon the lake's surface was met with dimpling rises all around. Could it be that the guy on the trail was here at a non-feeding time and didn't see any fish? Maybe he was using big spinners and was scorned by trout that were searching for smaller, more natural-looking food. Maybe he was being honest. This seemed less and less likely as late afternoon turned to evening and the rises went from sporadic to consistent, and then, as evening became dusk, the pace of the rising fish went from consistent to crazy. Trout were rising all over the lake everywhere I looked for the last hour of light; at times dozens were within casting range. I figured that it would be hard not to catch fish, and nearly impossible not to see them at this lake. I concluded that the line, "I only know about Purple Lake. Don't go there," could be translated as: "Purple is a great lake loaded with colorful, freely rising trout. I don't want you or anyone else to know about it. Please don't go there."

There was a heavy caddis hatch going on, and while a size 16 Elk Hair Caddis did acceptable duty, the fish seemed choosy at times. I attributed their selectivity more to the abundance of naturals than to fishing-pressure-induced wariness. The supposedly crowded lake was all mine on this July evening, and I found it easy to catch my fill of frisky mid-sized trout (I've never used that term before, but I guess I consider 9 to 11 inches to be mid-sized for high Sierra trout).

After catching a dozen in a couple of hours in the lake, I moved to the outlet creek. The action was similarly fast, with hungry hybrids in every piece of holding water. The creek trout are a bit smaller than those in the lake, topping out at 9 or 10 inches. The biggest challenge is finding holding water in this little creek that drops steeply into Cascade Valley where it joins Fish Creek. When a quiet hole is located, the trout will be there.

I had a tough time pulling myself away from the creek (the old 'one more good hole' mentality set in, as it often does when fishing trout-filled creeks), but I managed to leave with just enough daylight remaining to find a campsite. I hadn't planned on it, but in the dusk I ended up pitching my tent in the same spot that Bill and I had used years earlier. I was alone this time, which gave me time to reflect as I sat by the fire. I thought about the changes my life had undergone in those 16 years, but I was pleased to find that Purple Lake hadn't changed at all.

The next morning I woke up to find that the trout were at it again. Not trying too hard to resist taking a few casts before breakfast, it wasn't long before I'd caught a plump 11-incher; only then did it feel OK to pack up and hit the trail. As I hiked up and out of the Purple Lake basin, I paused at the top of the ridge, turned, gazed down, and bid a fond farewell to my old friend. "See you in 2013," I saluted, as I drank its cool water from my bottle and headed south.

Lake Virginia

My first visit to big, beautiful Lake Virginia was one I'm not likely to forget. I'd planned to stay and fish for half the day, but a tremendous thunderstorm sent me under cover for a couple of additional hours. While holed up under a downed tree, I recorded in my notebook: "There are worse places to spend a day than beside a golden trout lake—even in bad weather when fishing isn't practical." After the rain slacked off, the lightning was still too close to allow safe casting, so I huddled in my perfect little nest and cooked my dinner for lunch while keeping an eye out for rising trout.

I had looked forward to visiting Virginia for years, ever since I'd read that the state-record golden trout came from it, so a great deal of patience was

A well-fed Lake Virginia golden trout.

The goldens were planted annually from 1954-1989 to keep pace with the heavy use the lake received at that time. Planting has been reduced since then, with the lake receiving golden fingerlings only twice, in 1994 and 1997. Reproduction is considered fair to good, and it is hoped that the lake will be able to support itself through natural reproduction in the future. I'd like for that to be the case, but my 1997 experience at the lake revealed only planted fish. I caught them in two size ranges: 7- to 8-inch dull-colored goldens—a size expected from the 1994 plant, and beautifully marked 11- to 12-inch fish that were probably from the 1989 plant. I neither caught nor saw any bigger, smaller, or in between those sizes. Don't get me wrong, I wasn't at all dissatisfied with catching 12-inch goldens—I'd be content to catch them all day long.

The fish were spread thinly throughout the lake, with the trail side being the least productive. The trout exist in moderate quantities, which allows them ample food and good growth rates. I saw dozens of hoppers around the lake, and that's the fly that was the most productive for me.

If there is any reproduction in the lake, perhaps the mature fish move down into the outlet creek, as goldens often do. Silver Pass Creek contains goldens throughout its entire length. The creek fish are colorful wild trout that are plentiful and easy to catch (even with a broken-tipped fly rod—which I unfortunately had first-hand experience with). This attractive, chattering creek is crossed and followed often enough by the JMT in its short run to have made a favorable impression on me, and to rate high on my list of intimate golden trout creeks.

Any reluctance at leaving the brightly colored goldens of Silver Pass Creek will be forgotten quickly when you reach similar fishing on the North Fork of Mono Creek. This creek is a little bigger, and so are the trout, although they wear the colors of hybrids rather than of pure goldens. No matter, the creek is pretty and so are the trout. This is a sound trout stream that should give hours of enjoyment to anyone who likes to fish moving water. I seem to crave that type of fishing, but I didn't particularly enjoy most of my time along the creek. The problem was that I wasn't fishing most of the time during my stay. I was mostly under cover waiting out a thunderstorm. When I was fishing, I was just biding my time, making do with a broken fly rod until I could reach the resort at Lake Edison. During this temporary fishing lull, I had a chance to contemplate the beautiful country I'd seen that day, and noted that the national parks don't have a monopoly on great scenery.

Mono Creek

The trail follows full-flowing Mono Creek for about a mile before crossing it on a sturdy bridge. The creek drains a large area and is a major, though relatively unknown, Sierra waterway. This is probably due in part to its being outside of a national park, and in part to being named a 'creek' instead of a 'river.' This lower portion of creek, which the trail crosses a mile above Lake Edison, is home to a very healthy population of brown trout. Typical at 8 to 10 inches, the resident browns sometimes reach 12 inches in the best spots. Further upstream, rainbows are dominant, but down lower they are outnumbered by browns.

Overleaf: Mono Creek at the bridge crossing. One of the largest volume 'creeks' in the Sierra. Brown trout are found in almost every pocket of slow water.

Lake Edison is well known for harboring big wild browns that fatten up on hatchery rainbows; like the 27-pounder that was netted a few years back. If caught with a hook and line, it would have been the state record brown trout. Some of the big browns from the lake move into the creek to spawn. At that time, 18-inch-plus browns can be hooked in the creek with light fly tackle—a sporting proposition for sure (note that I said "hooked," not "landed"). If you happen to be taking a fall trip on the JMT and find yourself timing the spawning run out of Edison just right, it could very well be the highlight of your JMT fishing experience. I'm sure I'd rather catch a 20-inch trout on a fly in a creek than catch a 20-pounder trolling a reservoir, but since I've never done the latter, I guess it's purely conjecture on my part. Mono Creek is a high-quality trout stream that provides excellent angling for resident trout, with the added bonus of possibly catching one of the monsters that come up from the lake.

Memories of the enjoyable fishing on Mono Creek may be just the fuel you need for the next few miles. After crossing Mono Creek, the assault on Bear Ridge begins immediately. Bear Ridge is very well named, I think. No, I didn't see any bears, but it's a bear of a climb for sure. It's 2200 feet up, with no fishing opportunities and not many views to divert your attention. The hiking guide says there are 53 switchbacks on the climb, which I confirmed (counting switchbacks turned out to be my diversion—maybe it'll replace fly fishing as my new pastime...) This stretch is, understandably, one of the least-used sections of the JMT, because, in addition to the reasons above, good lateral trails sit at either end. I didn't see anybody else on this portion, and it was obviously less trodden and more overgrown than any other section; I think through-hikers are the only ones who use it.

Bear Creek

The reward for reaching the top of the ridge is beautiful Bear Creek. It's another full-flowing, major Sierra creek that abounds with trout. Golden, rainbow, hybrid, and brook trout are all in evidence in its trailside upper miles. The fish regularly reach 10 inches, and every good pocket and pool seems to hold a couple of that size. The creek features classically gorgeous water of all types; walking its banks is pure delight. I'm sure non-fishermen revel in its beauty, while mountain trout fishermen will be doubly enthralled with this high-country treasure of a trout stream.

As you hike and fish your way up Bear Creek, you'll step across the tiny Hilgard Branch. It's loaded with colorful goldens to 8 inches. It's a fun creek that's best enjoyed by those who hike along it as they head for Lake Italy and the other lakes it drains. For JMT hikers, I don't think it's worth spending the time that could be better spent fishing the main creek.

Just above the headwater forks of Bear Creek, the trail crosses, then follows, the West Fork. At the crossing, good numbers of golden and brook trout to 8 inches are found in the pockets. Upstream at idyllic Rosemarie Meadow, the fish, now mostly brook trout, are of similar sizes. This is a restful place, preferred by those who like to cast dry flies in open meadows to marked, rising trout.

Marie Lake

The preceding twenty miles of trail has predominantly featured stream fishing. Those who favor still water will be happy to reach Marie Lake, one of the biggest lakes on the entire trail (92 acres). It's a windy exposed lake that lies at the base of Seldon Pass at an elevation of 10,500 feet. Brook trout were planted in 1943, and have been reproducing for many decades. Golden trout have been planted numerous times since the 1920s, but haven't been successful at natural propagation. In 1997, I found no goldens surviving from the 1987 plant, and only fingerlings from the next plant—which had taken place just weeks before I arrived. Even the brook trout don't seem to be thriving, as much as merely surviving, at Marie. The population is sparse, but through diligent effort I found a half dozen brook trout in the 12- to 15-inch range on the southeastern side of the lake. Most were smaller, but the group I located were of an impressive size for trout living in a high-elevation lake. Marie Lake provides a pretty setting for those who stand on its shore, but it's really spectacular to look down upon from Seldon Pass, with the Mono Divide forming a sensational backdrop.

On the south side of Seldon Pass the trail follows an infant creek toward Heart Lake. This miniature creek gives a preview of the type of fishing that awaits the angler over the next several miles—fast action for plentiful, willing golden trout. The 5- to 8-inch goldens in the inlet creek occupy nearly every possible hold.

Heart Lake
Intimate Heart Lake is also full of goldens that get slightly bigger; commonly reaching 9 or 10 inches. I guess the lake has the potential to grow big fish, as 15-inch goldens were seen near the inlet in 1940 by a DFG survey team. Heart was originally stocked with trout from Golden Trout Creek in 1914. Reproduction is considered fair, and seems to be enough to sustain the lake without hatchery supplementation. The trout are evenly distributed around

The author at Seldon Pass (10,900 feet). Fly rod at the ready for the golden trout in the creeks and lakes below the pass.

the tiny lake, which only took me about a half hour to circle while casting. Very enjoyable fishing in a pleasant setting is the way I remember Heart Lake.

Sallie Keyes Lakes

If you liked Heart Lake, you'll love the Sallie Keyes Lakes. Again, golden trout are the quarry, and these twin lakes both have sizable populations of the well-named *salmo aguabonita*. The lakes were originally planted with goldens in 1914, again in 1928, and were last planted in 1985. Excellent natural reproduction conditions are present, so there may be no need to plant again. Together, the lakes and creek form a very healthy, self-sustaining golden trout fishery. The inlet creek to the upper lake doesn't have much holding water, but where there is a good hole, there will usually be a trout. I took plump, strong goldens to 10 inches in this little creek.

Both lakes teem with 8- to 10-inch goldens that rise by the hundreds on summer evenings. There is a small connector stream between the lakes, so the fish can move back and forth freely. The lower lake may have a few more fish, while the upper lake's fish may average an inch longer, but the differences are slight—overall the lakes are relatively interchangeable. I found several 10-inchers, and a few in the 11- to 12-inch range that rose to dry flies and put up a spirited fight. A trophy-sized golden is possible, as an 18-incher was seen in 1961. The small creek that connects the lakes is a productive spot to try during mid-day before the lakes come alive with rising trout.

These lakes are fairly well known for providing high-quality fishing and good camping, so they host many visitors. Their location, near a major pass, also adds to their popularity as a nice spot to rest either before or after making the big climb. This nice package is further enhanced by the surrounding beauty.

I met two different through-hikers, at different points along the trail, that had caught their only fish of their respective trips at the Sallie Keyes Lakes. They were both casual fishermen, admitting that they weren't too skillful, and each expressed a certain degree of dismay that they were successful at these lakes. This is one of those rare places where beginners can have a memorable time catching more and bigger wild trout than they thought possible, while experienced veterans find the fishing challenging and rewarding enough to captivate them for hours on end.

The fishery really does have it all: two lakes, a stone's throw away from each other (literally a stone's throw, it wouldn't hurt your arm even if you didn't warm up), and two inlet creeks—all full of 8- to 12-inch freely rising

A typical gaudily colored golden trout from the Sallie Keyes Lakes.

gorgeous wild trout. Throw in top-notch scenery and the remote location, and you have the makings of a golden trout Shangri-La.

When it leaves the Sallie Keyes Lakes, the trail runs near, but out of sight of, the outlet creek for a short distance. As expected, Sallie Keyes Creek is brimming with goldens, and is particularly pleasant to amble along about a half mile below the lake where it flows through a picturesque meadow.

If you're not tired of catching goldens in clear flowing water, Senger Creek is a delightful place to spend a few fishing minutes. It's another little jewel of a creek full of 5- to 8-inch iridescent goldens. The trout are so numerous that they can be caught right at the trail crossing. The creek was named for Joachim Henry Senger, one of the four original founders of the Sierra Club (along with John Muir, Warren Olney, and William Armes). By heading up or downstream, a dry-fly fisherman could have a super time catching dozens of goldens while fishing in pure solitude on water that goes unfished for years on end. Imagine owning a golden trout stream for the low price of a day's hike. Only in America, and only due to the far-sighted efforts of individuals like Senger who fought to protect and preserve these mountains for posterity.

South Fork of the San Joaquin River

As you descend into the drainage of the South Fork of the San Joaquin, you'll come to a trail junction that presents the following dilemma to purist JMT through-hikers: Do you go left down the official portion of trail, or do you go right to the luxurious natural pools of the Blayney Hot Springs? The Hot Springs are only a mile out of the way when the Florence Lake Trail is used to return to the JMT. Judging from the condition of each of the trails, I'd conclude that most hikers opt to deviate slightly from the official route and soak their weary muscles in warm water for perhaps the first time in weeks. The official stretch of trail doesn't offer any special incentive beyond solitude, as it is relatively viewless. The lack of traffic on the official portion of trail is furthered by the numerous hikers that take advantage of the mail drop service offered by the Muir Trail Ranch, which is near Blayney Hot Springs. The ranch is conveniently located at about the halfway point of the JMT, and doesn't require much of a deviation to reach, so its popularity as a re-supply post is assured.

Perhaps the only drawback to camping in the Hot Springs vicinity is its popularity—you certainly won't be alone. I found myself near a large group of Boy Scouts who were having a great time around the evening campfire. After so many nights camping alone in total silence, I was concerned about the interference of human sound keeping me awake, so I camped close to a rapid stretch of river, hoping to use the white water as white noise to drown out their camp.

As difficult as the trail branch decision may be for hiking purists, for the JMT hiker who's also a fisherman, it's an easy one. You see, to get to the Blayney Hot Springs you have to cross the South Fork, which just happens to hold outstanding brown trout. I'm not sure which I enjoyed more, the fishing or the hot bath. At the time I was nursing a sore knee, so I guess I was using alternating temperature therapy (cold/hot/cold) as I waded wet across the cold river, soaked in the hot spring, then waded back across the river to camp.

I gave up valuable evening fishing time while lounging in the hot springs. Rarely do I think any activity is worthwhile when it comes at the expense of prime fishing time (eating and sleeping included), but this was one exception

The author relaxing in a warm pool at Blayney Hot Springs. After a week or more on the trail, the warm water is a luxury to be savored – it's certainly worth the short detour from the trail.

that proved a worthy trade off. After ten days on the trail (at ten miles per day and 10,000 feet climbed), three days since my last cleansing swim, and with a sore knee, my one hour sacrifice of fishing time was very well spent. After an hour alone in the hot pool, I still had a hard time leaving—even as the best fishing time of the day was approaching. The only thing that forced me to leave the soothing water was knowing that I would need some daylight to negotiate the strong current while wading back across the river.

I'm not a connoisseur of hot tubs, but I've been in enough of them to know that I enjoy them—for awhile and to a point. However, no man-made hot tub, sauna, or spa that I've ever experienced could hold a candle to the natural hot spring pool that I luxuriated in that evening. Of course, I'd never been in an open-air hot tub, in the middle of a meadow, encircled by high peaks, alone, in total silence, having not bathed in days, having not felt warm water in over a week, and having taxed my muscles to their limit for ten straight days.

As I relaxed in the hot spring the serenity was overwhelming—it was a powerful moment for me. I couldn't help verbalizing a prayer of thanksgiving to God for all my blessings, especially the three that were waiting for me back at home. That evening I wrote in my notebook about the dichotomous pull of emotions: "It's strange realizing at once that I wouldn't want to be anywhere else in the world, and realizing that I miss my family and long to be with them. The solution, I guess, would be to take them with me, but that will have to wait until the kids can carry a pack (that's still several years off, I'm afraid, as baby Maggie hasn't learned to walk yet)." It was one of those spiritual times that I experience on a regular basis when hiking and fishing the Sierra backcountry, where I look skyward and say, "God, if you give us this on earth, I've just got to see your heaven."

Now, let's get out of the hot springs and into the cold water of the South San Joaquin. In the area of river near the hot springs, brown and rainbow trout are present, with the browns outnumbering and outgrowing the rainbows. The rainbows, on the small side at an average of 8 inches, are probably outnumbered 10-1 by the browns. The browns average size is a couple of inches longer (not 10 times as big, unfortunately), and enough of them reach the 12- to 14-inch range to provide exciting river fishing. I had a strike from a brown that looked even a little bigger as it rose from a deep hole to attack my hopper, but I missed the strike so its size was never confirmed.

As you move upstream, rejoining the JMT, the river comes in and out of view as the trail follows it toward Kings Canyon National Park. The large, fast river is usually within earshot—heard easily where its pace quickens—and with just a little bit of scrambling you can access seldom-fished stretches of water. By the time the border of Kings Canyon is reached, the numbers of rainbows are about equal to the browns. These are uncrowded miles of water that could withstand a great deal more fishing pressure. As it is now, there is an excellent population of trout, and I don't expect this high-class trout water to change due to overfishing because of the difficult access. This far upstream, the only visitors (on foot or on horseback) will be staying overnight—it's too far from road-ends for day trippers.

The water is also tough to cover—requiring a great deal of work in scrambling along its rocky, tree-lined banks. The river has a strong flow as it alternates between riffles, rocky runs, and pools. Wading in the strong current can be difficult until late season, at which time climbing over and around boulders is required. This water type has always been my absolute favorite. Choices abound as to what type of fishing to do: dry or

Hefty browns are found in the lower miles of the South Fork.

nymph, attractor or imitative, fast water or slow. Every bend in the river and each peek over the next rock reveals a new water type. When fishing the pocket water, choices of casting locations are seemingly endless. Since browns and rainbows are both present, the options are even greater, as there may be fish in both fast water and slow.

The fun really starts when a fish big enough to call the shots and take out line is hooked. With rocks and logs as obstacles and safe havens, and the strong current as its ally, the trout has a 50-50 chance of escape even if the fisherman makes all the right decisions. A foot-long fish can be a tough adversary in water like this. The same fish in a big broad, deep pool could be stripped in and landed at least 9 out of 10 times.

In this steep-gradient, freestone canyon river, fishing for wild trout is constantly changing, extremely sporting, and never dull. Factor in the uncrowded, scenic location, and the physical demands of the terrain, and you have the ingredients for a complete fishing experience. At the end of a day on water like this I am usually left with a warm glow of accomplishment no matter how many fish were caught.

The first time I fished the South Fork of the San Joaquin I knew immediately that it was my kind of water. After landing colorful, hard-fighting, foot-long browns and rainbows in the first two holes I tried, I felt the thrill that comes with discovery. This must be a similar feeling to that felt by miners when they find a rich vein. Walking back to camp for the night I also felt a little regret. The regret came from the realization that I'd fished the Sierra for twenty years before I discovered this rich vein of water. But the overwhelming emotion was of joy, the feeling that I'd made a new friend who said: "Drop by and see me any time you're in the area." I plan to do just that. I now have dozens of similar friends up and down the mountain range. The problem will be finding the time to keep in touch with them all. There are so many miles of quality fishing water on the South Fork—that are difficult enough to reach—that I'm not worried about squatters overrunning my claim. There's enough color in this strike for all hard-working trout fishermen to share without hurting the quality or character of the experience.

Piute Creek

At the border of Kings Canyon National Park, Piute Creek is reached just above its confluence with the South Fork of the San Joaquin. Piute is another big creek that drains a large high-country region. At the entrance to the park, Piute Creek is crossed by the trail on a sturdy steel bridge—a welcome sight after many wet crossings. If not for this bridge, early and mid-season fords would be difficult, time consuming, and dangerous, as the creek moves quickly over the steep terrain.

The water is nice to look at, but from a fishing standpoint it's not ideal. The downside is the lack of holding water, but where it can be located, good

numbers of trout are found. In the immediate vicinity of the bridge there are only a handful of good holes.

The trout in this stretch range from pure rainbows that have made the short, steep climb up from the San Joaquin, to the nearly pure goldens— like the 9-inch beauty I caught just below the bridge. Most of the fish are hybrids of the two, and, regardless of type, average about 8 inches. I've seen a few in the

Wading the South Fork of the San Joaquin River.

10- to 12-inch class, but to catch them consistently, you've got to seek out the more promising casting spots by scrambling up or downstream. There are also a few brook trout present, which add even more variety to the wide range of colors presented by the inter-breeding rainbows and goldens. Catching pretty trout from a pretty creek in pretty surroundings is a pretty nice combination.

KINGS CANYON
NATIONAL PARK, NORTH

Entering a national park always feels good, largely because the most spectacular land of all is found in these special places. When you cross the bridge over Piute Creek you enter Kings Canyon National Park. The landscape doesn't change immediately of course, but just the fact that there is a sturdy bridge over the rushing creek is one of the indicators that you're in a national park. Bridges and trails are both usually better maintained inside the parks. For a fisherman, it's nice to be where there are well established, stable, wild-trout populations that have thrived virtually unchanged for decades, and promise to remain in that state without man's intervention. Kings Canyon and Sequoia both stopped the practice of planting trout in 1977, so today, all trout found will be wild fish that have been born in the water in which they live.

Kings Canyon became a national park rather recently. All the pieces came together after years of effort on behalf of the Sierra Club and others, and the park was formed in 1940. The result is perpetual protection for some of the best wilderness land in the high Sierra. Kings Canyon has the distinction of claiming a longer stretch of the JMT than any other wilderness area—over one third of the trail, 75 miles, runs through it. The park is uncrossed and virtually untouched by roads, so to see its finest treasures you must be willing to walk. Fishing the Kings Canyon backcountry is usually an uncrowded proposition carried out in a variety of water types, and can be very good.

Now that the planting of trout has been stopped, it's safer to fish the wilderness lakes. Let me explain that statement. I was talking to a longtime backcountry ranger in Kings Canyon who passed along a humorous incident. He was on the shore of a remote lake many years ago, when a plane flew overhead to carry out an air drop of fingerling trout. He said he was about 25 feet from the lake, but still was hit by a few of the errant fish. He was unhurt by the little trout, and was happy to report that most of the fish hit the water and survived. Just be on the lookout for low-flying planes when you're fishing a lake that is on the fish-stocking schedule. The national parks are now safe from that hazard.

South Fork of the San Joaquin River

If you're heading south and didn't deviate from the trail in the Blayney Hot Springs area, up to this point the South Fork of the San Joaquin may have provided only distant murmurs and fleeting glimpses, rather than thrashing strikes from hungry browns. Don't worry though, the trail follows the river closely for the next four miles, where the South Fork offers a hospitable welcome to Kings Canyon National Park. The water comes into close view and will tempt all but the most hurried hiking fishermen. This is high-quality water in beautiful unspoiled condition that cries out 'Fish

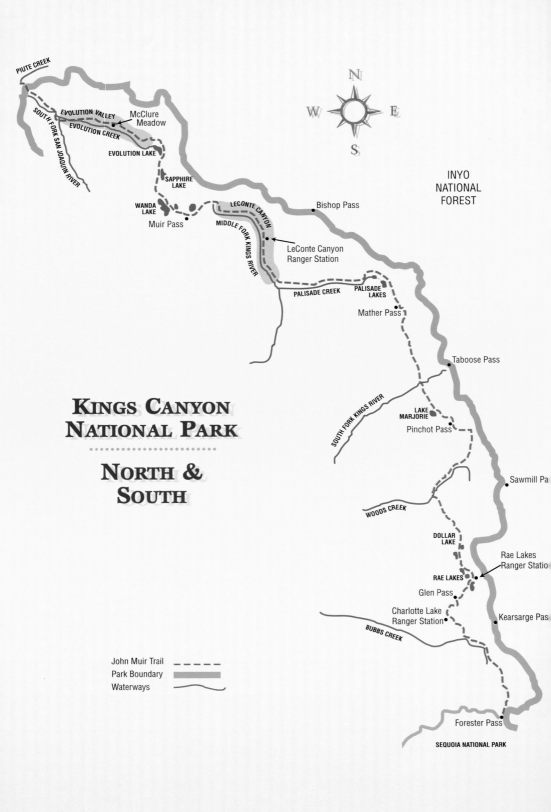

PIUTE CREEK

EVOLUTION VALLEY

McClure
Meadow

EVOLUTION CREEK

SOUTH FORK SAN JOAQUIN RIVER

EVOLUTION LAKE

SAPPHIRE
LAKE

WANDA
LAKE

LECONTE CANYON

Muir Pass

MIDDLE FORK KINGS RIVER

Bishop Pass

LeConte Canyon
Ranger Station

PALISADE CREEK

PALISADE
LAKES

Mather Pass

Taboose Pass

INYO
NATIONAL
FOREST

N
W   E
S

SOUTH FORK KINGS RIVER

LAKE
MARJORIE

Pinchot Pass

Sawmill Pa

KINGS CANYON
NATIONAL PARK

NORTH &
SOUTH

WOODS CREEK

DOLLAR
LAKE

Rae Lakes
Ranger Statio

RAE LAKES

Glen Pass

Charlotte Lake
Ranger Station

Kearsarge Pas

BUBBS CREEK

John Muir Trail
Park Boundary
Waterways

Forester Pass

SEQUOIA NATIONAL PARK

me!' The angler that doesn't answer this call in the affirmative is a jaded individual indeed.

Where the river is first reached, just outside of Kings Canyon, rainbows and browns to 12 inches are common. Every likely hole appears to hold a couple in the 10- to 12-inch range, and sometimes a bigger brown is spotted. The river seems to be in a hurry to leave the mountains, so in the first half of the season good holding water is hard to find. From mid-summer through fall, when its level drops, the South Fork is in its prime as a fly-fishing river. This is the most enjoyable time to probe its waters, searching the pools, runs, and endless pockets for spirited trout.

Upstream in Kings Canyon, you'll notice the rainbows start to take on a golden color. These (G-RB) hybrids are similar in size to the rainbows downstream, and share the same niche in the river system. The range of the brown trout extends about to Aspen Meadow where, just above, big cascades halt their upstream progress. The absence of browns leaves the river to the hybrids and to pure-looking golden trout in the 8- to 11-inch range. The trout rarely exceed 12 inches up at this 8500-foot elevation. Fine fishing for colorful trout continues for miles upstream, but the JMT leaves the South Fork at the foot of Goddard Canyon, crossing it on a sturdy bridge.

Evolution Valley: Evolution Creek

As difficult as it may be to leave the outstanding fishing of the South Fork of the San Joaquin, the promise of unsurpassed spectacular alpine splendor should serve as ample incentive to draw the hiker up the steep ridge to Evolution Valley. When the subject of hiking the JMT is broached among mountain enthusiasts, Evolution Valley is often cited as one of the scenic climaxes. When you consider all the grandeur that the trail passes through, this is high praise indeed. If you're fortunate enough to see Evolution Valley, I doubt you'll be disappointed—it's one of those rare places that exceeds even the highest expectations no matter how exaggerated the descriptions or how glowing the recommendations have been.

As you proceed uphill, Evolution Creek will be heard crashing down toward its terminus with the South San Joaquin. The waterfalls and cascades soon come into view, beckoning the angler and sightseer alike to leave the trail for a closer look. The large holes in this rough stretch contain some of the biggest fish in the creek—healthy goldens in the 10- to 12-inch range.

The terrain flattens as the trail enters Evolution Valley near Evolution Meadow. This is an ideal spot to stop for lunch and some dry-fly fishing. It's possible to take dozens of little goldens on almost any small fly anywhere in the meadow—even right where the trail makes a wet crossing of the creek. An Elk Hair Caddis (#16-18) works great when the meadow is full of little tan hoppers—I was getting a trout on nearly every cast. The 5- to 8-inch goldens were lying in wait along grassy edges, gorging on unfortunate hoppers that were blown into the water. The growing season is short above 9000 feet, so the trout were taking full advantage of the feast laid out before them. The same applies to the visitor, who should make the most of the opportunity and take time to enjoy the hard-earned visual feast.

The gentle stroll upstream affords some terrific views of the little side

Overleaf: One of the impressive falls of Evolution Creek below Evolution Valley.

canyon creeks cascading down the walls of the valley. The trail stays far enough from the creek that the fisherman in the group won't quite be able to see rising trout, and thus be tempted to slow everyone's progress while he takes, "just a few casts here."

Most fishermen don't leave the trail to seek out the creek, but rather wait until the two again join in McClure Meadow. The fishing in this big, beautiful meadow is almost identical to that of Evolution Meadow. Namely, competent fly-casters can effortlessly catch their fill of colorful 5- to 8-inch golden trout all day long. This is one of the rare spots where it's hard for even a dedicated angler to concentrate fully on fishing due to the distraction of the awe-inspiring scenery. The best way to sum up the surrounding beauty is to quote what John Glenn said when looking down at the earth from outer space: "To look out at this kind of creation out here and not believe in God is, to me, impossible. It just strengthens my faith." I feel that those words apply to McClure Meadow in specific, and to the entire JMT in general. McClure Meadow gets my vote as the best of Evolution Valley. Imagine a big, long meadow, pine trees at the margins, with high, bright granite walls on each side and several of the tallest peaks in North America majestically standing at the head. Add a crystal-clear stream flowing through tall green grass, with golden trout dimpling the surface, and you have luscious McClure Meadow.

As the trail follows Evolution Creek upstream, it passes intimate, beautiful Colby Meadow where the creek remains full of smallish goldens that can

Wading Evolution Creek below The Hermit.

53

*Evolution Creek puts on a great
waterfall display during runoff time.*

be caught with relative ease. At the head of Evolution Valley, the Darwin Canyon Branch of Evolution Creek is crossed. The fishing prospects in this branch are no different than in the main creek, with 6- to 8-inch goldens thriving to the point of over-population.

Evolution Lake

Upon leaving the Darwin Canyon Branch, the trail climbs to the lakes of the Evolution Basin. At one mile long and two miles high, Evolution Lake greets the hiker with a continuation of stunning scenery. Surrounded by 12,000- and 13,000-foot peaks, and full of golden trout, the lake is, understandably, a popular overnight stop. It was planted with goldens initially in 1928, then several times until the last plant in 1963. Reproduction is excellent, so planting is no longer needed. The goldens are so successful at reproducing that their numbers are high, which keeps their average size low. I've taken a couple of gorgeous 10-inch trout, but most are about 7 inches. I found the Evolution Lake goldens to be the prettiest in the area, with exceptionally bright orange bellies highlighting their colors.

Above Evolution Lake, Evolution Creek continues to accommodate a dense golden trout population. The marvelous setting and the creek's big holes make for an enjoyable fishing stretch up to Sapphire Lake.

Sapphire Lake

The JMT borders the entire west shore of Sapphire Lake. Scenically, this precious jewel is similar to Evolution Lake—which means it's an extraordinary place. The trout population is also similar to that of Evolution Lake, with the excellent natural reproduction in evidence as a thousand rising trout bear witness to it on most summer evenings. Also like Evolution, the goldens at

Trout Fishing the JOHN MUIR TRAIL

Sapphire top out at 10 inches, but their average size is slightly bigger here. The trout put up a spirited struggle when hooked, seeming to be stronger and better conditioned than their neighbors down the hill. Time after time I'd be playing a trout that I was sure would be 10 to 12 inches, only to land it and find another 8-inch overachiever. If the fishing is slow during the day, try the head of the lake where the broad shallow inlet creek usually holds a large concentration of actively feeding trout.

An unusually wide range of food sizes is available to these trout. Stomach samples revealed that hundreds of tiny (#30) green midges were being taken by each fish, and I saw big (#6) orange hoppers as I walked the shore. I found more success with small flies—the smaller the better—during the late afternoon and evening rises.

To illustrate the quantity of trout in Sapphire, I'll describe a game I played one evening after arriving late at the lake. I imagined that I was without food and had to catch my dinner. With one hour until dark, the pressure was on to avoid going to sleep with an empty stomach. I figured I'd need about four of the plump 7- to 8-inch goldens to satisfy my energy needs. I caught the four in ten minutes, easily winning the game I'd set up. After releasing the fish, (that should have been grateful I was only playing a game), I went back to camp where I enjoyed a big rice stew without the bother of cleaning fish.

Sapphire Lake is mediocre as a camping destination, being treeless, exposed, and windy. I stayed there anyway, and was rewarded with a superb star display. It wasn't anything extraordinary like a meteor shower, it was just a tremendously

Casting amidst wildflowers at Evolution Lake.

Darwin Canyon Creek and Mt. Lamarck.

clear night; perfect for stargazing. I don't remember ever seeing so many stars, or such a large, distinct Milky Way. The night was cloud free, with only the tiniest sliver of a moon, and at 11,000 feet, I'd never camped any closer to the stars.

Above Sapphire Lake, the trail passes a couple of unnamed lakes that sit below Mt. Huxley. For the most part, they're barren, although I did see one trout in the creek just below them. It is possible that in good water years a few fish could work up from Sapphire Lake, but I doubt they'd survive a winter in these shallow lakes that are likely prospects for winterkill. The stream below them is also very shallow and swift, so I doubt it would be accommodating to year-round residents.

The next lake reached is one of the biggest on the entire JMT. The trail follows its east shore closely, so you get a good look at the water. Long, wide Wanda Lake looks promising, but is virtually fishless. Let me explain what the word 'virtually' means in this case. On my first trip to this 11,400-foot-high lake I found it 25% iced over (I was just in time for the spring thaw on August 19th). I've cast all along the lake on two visits, and haven't caught anything. I was about to conclude that it was barren, which is what I'd been told, when I received an unexpected surprise. Using stealth usually reserved for lakes with trout in them, I crept out from behind a boulder and cast my hopper at the head of the lake where an inlet creek trickles in. Immediately, two huge goldens bolted to open water. I got a great look at them as they swam parallel to shore directly in front of me in shallow water, taunting me with their size and beauty. In the crystal-clear water I could see the thick red-orange lateral stripe of the male half of the spawning pair. As I write this, months later, I can still see that trout's colors. With stunned disbelief, I froze slack-jawed, and conservatively estimated their sizes at 15 and 16 inches. I would never know their exact sizes, as I never saw them again.

With renewed vigor I stepped up my search of the shoreline, but never saw another fish. After much thought, I concluded that I may have seen the only two fish in the lake. I don't think I was given erroneous information from the

56

Wanda Lake at ice-out in August. Spring thaw arrives late at 11,400 feet.

sources that had told me Wanda was fishless—I think it usually is. I happened to be there during an extremely big water year; a rare occasion when the tiny inlet creek was flowing. The creek is probably dry during most years, in fact, it isn't even shown on some maps. The two trout most likely came down from the lake above (which does contain golden trout), and found themselves in a virtual trout paradise. They had a monopoly on all the food in this huge lake, which includes plenty of frogs and plentiful aquatic insects such as black caddis and green stoneflies. It was as if they were Columbus and had discovered the new world, only better—this one was uninhabited. When I saw them they were in the midst of finding the only bump in their road to Shangri-La. The very creek that had delivered them to this land of milk and honey (land of frogs and stoneflies?) was betraying their efforts at reproduction. The creek was too small for them to re-enter, so they were left to spawn unsuccessfully in the lake. My guess is that they will die old, big, and lonely.

This scenario may occur from time to time, but usually the lake is devoid of trout. Even if there are a few fish in Wanda, it's so big that trying to find them would be like looking for a needle in a haystack (or, as I have tried, looking for a size 24 hook in shag carpeting). I was fortunate to see the big goldens, but I didn't even come close to catching them. An angler with a little bit of luck, a little bit of skill, and the patience of Job might be able to hang the trout of a lifetime, but I can't recommend Wanda Lake as a prime fishing stop.

Perched immediately above Wanda Lake is little Lake McDermand which was named for "Mr. Golden Trout," the late Charles McDermand, author of the 1946 book *Waters of the Golden Trout Country*. I was entertained and enthralled by his stories early in my Sierra trout-fishing career, and recommend it to anyone who can find a copy of the long-since out of print classic. Many of the DFG employees and other outdoor workers I meet in the Sierra were influenced as youngsters by that book. Appropriately, Lake McDermand does contain golden trout, but I'm sorry to say that the fishing can only be rated as fair at best. The trout are about average sized for lake-dwelling goldens, 7 to 11 inches, but their numbers are small. Still, Charlie would probably be pleased with the scenic

The Muir Hut at Muir Pass (11,955 feet).

location of his namesake, as it sits at the base of Muir Pass, sandwiched between lakes named for John Muir's two daughters, Wanda and Helen.

The often snow-covered struggle up to 12,000-foot Muir Pass is worthwhile, paying dividends to the hiker with spectacular views in every direction. There is a stone hut that sits atop the pass that's so tastefully constructed it doesn't seem to be an intrusion on the wilderness experience. The plaque on the hut reads: "To John Muir, lover of The Range of Light. This shelter was erected through the generosity of George Frederick Schwarz. 1931. Sierra Club. U.S. Forest Service." The Muir Hut is a pleasant place for lunch on a cold, windy day, and would be a welcome sight or could be a life-saving shelter, for someone caught near the top of the pass during a snowstorm.

If you can, do a big favor for a future traveler by bringing up a little piece of wood to place inside, near the fireplace. Someday, someone may thank you for it through chattering teeth as their hands and toes escape frostbite due to your thoughtfulness. I found a few sticks in a small pile on the floor, but no matches, so I left a couple. If you do decide to bring up some wood, make sure you plan it well in advance, as there is hardly a tree in sight when standing on the pass and looking in either direction of the trail. The pass region is encircled by 13,000-foot peaks, so have your camera handy.

On the south side of Muir Pass the trail passes large Helen Lake. Like sister lake Wanda, I'd been told that Helen was fishless, but in this case, I saw nothing to disprove the assertion. In 1997, a survey team studying the Sierra frog population gill-netted the lake and found no fish. It was planted with goldens eight times between 1928 and 1972, but they haven't been able to reproduce. In 1977, a park service group studying trout populations in Kings-Sequoia lakes saw only one fish in Helen, a golden of 18 inches. They surmised that since the lake doesn't provide conditions for reproduction, this solitary trout was the last survivor from the 1972 plant. It may have been the last fish ever to live in Helen Lake. The next few little tarns that the trail passes to the south should be skipped as they are also fishless.

Middle Fork of the Kings River

The next fishing opportunity comes in the tiny creek that the trail follows down from Muir Pass. The creek starts picking up tributaries in little Big Pete Meadow, becoming more of a river in big Little Pete Meadow (that's right, Big Pete Meadow is smaller than Little Pete Meadow—a full explanation is given in the book, *Place Names of the Sierra Nevada*). At this point, the little creek has become the Middle Fork of the Kings River, and the trout population is high all through LeConte Canyon. In the quiet water of Little Pete Meadow you're likely to see dozens of risers. This meadow was the site of an early golden trout planting effort. Those goldens interbred with rainbows, but there is still plenty of colorful evidence of their ancestry in their hybridized progeny.

The river abounds with 6- to 10-inch trout—some look like pure goldens, some like pure rainbows, and the rest take on every possible color combination in between. In addition to the beautiful trout, this is a classically gorgeous stretch of river, flowing through forests and meadows, surrounded by towering cliffs and 13,000-foot peaks. LeConte Canyon is sometimes cited by JMT through-hikers as a favorite spot, taking a back seat only to Evolution Valley. If you happen to approach LeConte Canyon from the Dusy Basin, you'll gain an appreciation of its depth as you're treated to astounding views into the river canyon.

The trail crosses the tiny Dusy Branch below Little Pete Meadow. Although this branch is loaded with hybrids, it really isn't worthy of taking fishing time away from the Middle Fork. Holding water is scarce and the trout range from small to tiny. You can find 8-inch fish in the prime holes, but the majority of fishable spots are full of barely hookable 4- to 5-inch trout.

The JMT follows the dashing river for a few more miles to spacious, enticing Grouse Meadow—a picturesque spot where the oft-rising trout seem to call out for dry flies. The fish can be tough to approach in the calm, clear meadow water, but the trout population is high and the angling is idyllic. The hybrids are easier to fool both above and below Grouse Meadow in

the pocket water—if the angler doesn't mind scrambling and rock hopping. I enjoy both types of fishing, so my hiking progress is slowed by the variety of water types. Trout size is fairly constant all the way through LeConte Canyon; the fish rarely exceed 10 inches and average about 7.

Palisades

After the pleasant amble through the canyon, the trail leaves the delightful Middle Fork of the Kings to head east up Palisade Creek. It's tough to say goodbye to this enjoyable river, but there is some consolation in the fact that Palisade Creek offers similarly fine angling all the way up to the Palisade Lakes. The only regrettable point becomes obvious all too soon, though. Instead of strolling gently downhill along the Middle Fork, you now have to earn your steps as you climb steeply uphill. Rest breaks become more entertaining (though less restful) when you discover the dense population of trout in the nearby creek. The trout are about the same size as those in the Middle Kings, with 8- to 10-inchers abundantly inhabiting this charming creek.

After a few miles, the trail crosses a small creek that drains the Palisade Basin, and which holds 6- to 8-inch goldens. Similar-sized goldens are found just past Deer Meadow in multi-branched Glacier Creek. Neither creek warrants much of the angler's attention when compared to Palisade Creek, but both may be worth a few quick casts during a rest stop if your rod is handy. There are pretty goldens waiting for your dry flies in every likely spot.

Soon after crossing Glacier Creek, the trail steepens while Palisade Creek becomes less fishworthy as it cascades down the Golden Staircase. After the long climb, Lower Palisade Lake is a welcome sight. The Palisade Lakes (Lower and Upper) and their surrounding peaks make for a top-notch alpine setting. Couple the scenery with their convenient location as a rest stop between steep climbs, and it's easy to figure the lakes' popularity with campers. Still, the Palisade Lakes seldom get crowded because they're a long way from trailheads. The fact that they offer fine fishing for golden trout is an added bonus that may make these lakes the highlight of your trip through the Kings Canyon stretch of the JMT.

Both lakes were planted with goldens numerous times in the 1950s, 60s, and 70s. The last plant was in 1973, so the thriving current population is evidence of a healthy self-sustaining fishery in both lakes. There is some interbreeding going on, as hybrids are present, but the majority of the fish strongly resemble golden trout. The populations are substantial in both lakes, as well as in the creek above, below, and between the lakes.

In many ways the Palisade Lakes remind me of the Sallie Keyes Lakes. Both areas feature plenty of golden trout in the 8- to 12-inch range, both offer two lakes to choose from, and both provide good nearby stream fishing.

Lower Palisade holds slightly bigger fish than Upper Palisade—trout that top out at about a foot long. Most of your catch at either lake will probably be 8 to 10 inches, and will surely be colorful. These lakes are definitely prime candidates for a layover day for anglers and non-anglers alike. The next dozen miles of trail includes two passes higher than 12,000 feet, so, with that in mind, a layover day at the Palisade Lakes might look even more attractive.

Opposite page: The Middle Fork of the Kings River in delightful LeConte Canyon.

KINGS CANYON
NATIONAL PARK, SOUTH

South Fork of the Kings River

From Upper Palisade Lake, it's a short, steep climb to Mather Pass (12,100 feet), which provides awesome views off either side. As the trail levels out from its descent on the south side to enter the Upper Basin, it follows a little creek that doesn't look particularly noteworthy. In fact, these are the headwaters of an extraordinary river, the South Fork of the Kings, which has attained worldwide fame downstream, where it carves out beautiful Kings Canyon. Just downstream from the park boundary, the South Fork joins the Middle Fork of the Kings to form the deepest canyon in North America— 8200 feet from river to mountain top.

John Muir wrote glowingly about the canyon of the South Fork of the Kings, in his 1891 article for *Century* magazine, "A Rival of the Yosemite," describing it as " . . . a veritable song of God." He was so impressed with the region that he called for its immediate preservation, saying: "Let our lawgivers then make haste, before it is too late, to save this surpassingly glorious region for the recreation and well-being of humanity, and the world will rise

A large, colorful golden trout – the highlight of a high-country fishing trip.

up and call them blessed." Thus, the wheels were set in motion for the creation of Kings Canyon National Park, which wouldn't be completed during Muir's lifetime, but the fruit grower from Martinez, California had planted the seed that gave birth to the park we enjoy today.

As you can see, the little trickle at your feet on the south side of Mather Pass is no ordinary Sierra creek. It's nice to keep this in mind as you jump across the tiny creek several times while following the trail in the Upper Basin.

The South Fork provides good fishing all the way down to Kings Canyon and beyond. In its extreme upper reaches along the JMT, the plentiful trout are goldens that average 7 inches. It's amazing how goldens look like rocks in these waters—shining and flashing in the sun. More than once I've spent time casting over a rock that I thought was a trout. Also, sometimes I was startled when the reverse would happen, and a rock would come to life right in front of me.

At the final crossing, where the trail leaves the river after following it for five miles, the goldens grow to a nice size, commonly reaching 9 or 10 inches. This crossing is the lowest point in elevation for many miles in either direction (although it's still over 10,000 feet) so it's a nice place for a cleansing dip.

As I was crossing the river I came across a couple of through-hikers, a father and son, who watched me intently as I fished. I made several casts in the closest few holes, plucked colorful, feisty goldens out of each likely spot, and made an impression on the fifteen-year-old spin fisherman. With a look of startled disbelief, he couldn't contain himself and had to vocalize his thoughts, "You just caught four fish!...That's how many I've caught in 10 days on the whole trip...I've seen people fly fishing before...I thought it was just waving the rod back and forth...I've never seen anyone catch a fish doing it." After explaining the fundamentals of fly fishing, I left him with a few flies and some instructions on how to best use them with a spinning rod.

As I headed upstream to try a few more holes, I couldn't help recalling a day when I was on the other end of a similar experience. I had just celebrated my fifteenth birthday on a family vacation to Yellowstone. The next day we hiked to a little creek that we'd been told contained cutthroat trout. After ignoring the grizzly bear footprints on the trail (or pretending to each other that we didn't see them), we arrived at the creek and were pleased to see that indeed, it held plenty of trout. My brother and I worked hard but couldn't draw a strike to our lures in the brushy creek. Just when we thought the fish were uncatchable, an obvious veteran of many a trout stream strolled into sight with a pipe in one hand and a fly rod in the other. We watched in awe as he pulled two hefty trout out of the very spots we'd just tried. Our trip was drawing to a close, so we had to wait until we returned home to buy fly rods and begin to learn how to use them. It would be several years (and a lot of rounds of golf) before I was successful at pulling "uncatchable" trout of my own out of a mountain stream, but the fly-fishing spark turned into a flame on that little stream in the mountains of a western national park. As I worked up the South Kings, I thought that perhaps on this day, in a different stream, in a different western national park, another fly fisherman was born at age 15. For his sake I hoped so, as in my opinion, fly fishing is the most enjoyable way to fish—especially in the mountains where it opens up the innumerable delightful little creeks that I've found endless pleasure exploring.

As the trail climbs out of the South Fork of the Kings drainage toward

Pinchot Pass, it crosses a few little creeks and skirts several unnamed lakelets. The creeks are shallow and hold a smattering of small golden trout, while the lakes abound with brook trout. This is a fun, uncrowded place to fish, particularly if you don't care about fish size—a veritable small-trout mecca. This area wouldn't be my choice for a fishing destination, but it is a nicer place to camp than the more exposed Lake Marjorie.

The brookies in these intimate lakes are easy marks for any method of angling, so they provide relaxing evening entertainment for campers who are recharging their batteries for the next day's climb over Pinchot Pass. I didn't employ this strategy on my first trip through the area, opting instead to climb Mather and Pinchot passes on the same day. They're only 9 1/2 miles apart, but in retrospect, I have to wonder what I was thinking in deciding to go over two of the three highest passes on the entire JMT in one day. The hiking component of that day certainly didn't leave much time for fishing, but I made up for it the next day by spending more time on the water than on the trail.

The trail borders broad Lake Marjorie before steepening in earnest and heading for Pinchot Pass. Marjorie is a stark, desolate, windy lake that offers only mediocre camping, but is full of willing brook trout that are well distributed all around the lake. The fish don't get too big at this high lake (11,132 feet), and are disappointingly pale. One 7-inch brookie I caught had virtually no color, looking like a hatchery rainbow or maybe like a Dolly Varden trout.

Upon leaving high-altitude Lake Marjorie, the trail heads higher still, for another 12,100-foot pass. Pinchot Pass was named for John Muir's nemesis Gifford Pinchot, the chief of the US Forest Service and a strong proponent of the 'multiple-use' concept of forestry management. Perhaps Muir would be pleased to know that the pass that bears Pinchot's name is rather unattractive on the north side where it's surrounded by brownish-red mountains instead of the usual bright white granite that distinguishes the high Sierra. For Mr. Pinchot's sake, at least the south side of the pass is nice—worthy of a photo for sure.

Twin Lakes

It's all downhill from Pinchot Pass to Twin Lakes, a fact that I was happy about after crossing the second 12,000-foot pass of the day. After I set up camp in a sheltered mini pine grove near Lower Twin Lake, I got out my maps and did a little figuring. The results explained why I was dragging a bit by afternoon—I'd covered 43 miles in 56 hours while fishing hard at every piece of water I encountered. I sarcastically wrote in my journal "An average of less than one mile per hour and I'm sore?" So much for enjoying every step and smelling the roses along the way.

The Twin Lakes proved to be good hosts to this tired hiker who was anxious to take off the pack and catch a few fish. As trail weary as I was, I still managed to get the tent set up in time to sample the fishing for the last half hour of light. Fortunately the lake was alive with rising trout, so I didn't have to walk far or work hard to hook up. In that half hour I landed six colorful brook trout and counted twenty missed strikes.

The next morning I was able to do a thorough search and survey of shallow, tiny Lower Twin Lake, and found that the prior night's brief encounter was an accurate representation of the fishing. The lake has a dense population

Trout Fishing the JOHN MUIR TRAIL

in my journal when I'm climbing passes. I wonder why? I guess the added physical strain increases the blood flow to my brain, which helps me think more clearly, allowing me to come up with more ideas...yeah, that sounds good, I'll go with that explanation.

After descending from Glen Pass, many people choose to take a short detour to camp at Charlotte Lake. The lake was planted with rainbows numerous times in the 1950s. Ancestors from those plants continue to exist in the lake, where there is a fair number of smallish rainbows that rarely exceed 10 inches.

Another lake that was previously a popular detour for JMT hikers is Bullfrog Lake. Suffering from overuse, this scenic lake is now closed to camping. It contains brook trout, but they are neither large enough nor numerous enough to justify a side trip to the lake just for the fishing. But I've included it here because if camping is permitted in the future, Bullfrog Lake will surely again be a popular spot—its location as the closest lake to the JMT south of Glen Pass will ensure that.

Bubbs Creek

The JMT leaves the loop trail and its legions of hikers at Bubbs Creek. The loop trail branches off downstream, while we head up Bubbs Creek. The trail follows this attractive creek for many miles, staying close enough for the hiker to see it alternately flow gently through meadows, and crash over small waterfalls.

There are substantial numbers of several different types of trout all along this stretch. Near Vidette Meadow you'll find an occasional brown in the 8- to 10-inch range, but they don't extend much further upstream. The creek is dominated here by hybrids, and also holds brook trout, while the upstream portion is all golden trout. The goldens come quickly and easily in the tempting meadows and plunge pools. Most are only 6 to 8 inches, but there are a few of 10 or 11 inches, which approaches trophy size for golden trout—especially creek-resident goldens. I can still picture one I caught of that size leaping high above its little pool with gold sides flashing in the sunlight. This was a fat, happy, hard-fighting, beautifully marked golden that impressed me as much as any sub 12-inch trout ever has. Bubbs Creek has a lot going for it as a trout stream, and should be a part of every passing angler's day.

The creek that drains Center Basin is also full of willing goldens. After crossing this little creek, you can put your rod away in preparation for the climb up to Forester Pass, the highest pass on the JMT (also the highest on the Pacific Crest Trail). As the trail steepens, Bubbs Creek no longer holds trout, nor do the lakes that dot the trailside.

As I headed up Forester Pass for the first time, I made some calculations (which could be filed under "Things you think about on the trail to keep your mind off the climb"). Using my eyes as a sextant, I figured I netted about five feet of elevation gain for every twenty steps on the well-graded switchbacks. At this rate (three inches of elevation gained per step, four steps to the foot), the climb of 3700 feet from Bubbs Creek to the top of the pass would take 14,800 steps. After arriving at that figure I thought perhaps it would have been better not to know. A week earlier I did count the switchbacks up relatively viewless Bear Ridge, but I decided not to count my steps up Forester Pass in favor of concentrating on the scenery.

As I reached the much-anticipated top, the view was great, even as the dense clouds thickened. While catching my breath it started to hail. "Right on time," I thought, "after all, what would a pass be without hail." The hail turned to snow, prompting me to curtail my rest break, take a final look back at Kings Canyon National Park and head for Sequoia. Halfway down the south side of the pass, the skies began to clear and the highest peaks in the continental United States unfolded before me.

Forester Pass (13, 180 feet). The highest pass on the John Muir Trail, and the highest point on the Pacific Crest Trail.

SEQUOIA NATIONAL PARK

Sequoia National Park is truly a remarkable piece of earth—a land of superlatives. The park contains the highest mountain in the contiguous United States, 14,494-foot Mt. Whitney. Established in 1890, Sequoia is the second oldest national park in the United States. The early distinction was based largely on the desire of conservationists to protect the world's largest trees.

The Giant Forest of sequoia trees was explored and named by John Muir in 1875, and includes the approximately 2,500-year-old General Sherman Tree—the world's largest living thing. As you stand at its base and look up through its mighty branches, it's hard to imagine that this tree was about 500 years old, and already huge, in the time of Jesus Christ.

The fishing regulations for Sequoia are the same as those for Kings Canyon. The parks are dually managed, so their planting histories are also similar, with planting stopped at each in 1977.

Below Forester Pass

The unnamed lakes south of Forester Pass are devoid of fish life, but they still provided me with a fishing adventure of sorts. I was hopping down some talus to scout out one of the big lakes to the east of the trail when my foot slipped. The fateful step was onto a 30-degree downward slanting rock—the type of step that had been successfully carried out hundreds of times that day, and thousands of times in the past. The rocks were slick from rain, but I don't feel I was hurrying carelessly. I landed with my left leg crossed underneath my body, and I came down on it with the full weight of myself and my pack. For a while I was sure I'd broken my ankle. I did a quick calculation and estimated that I would have to hobble approximately 26.2 miles to the nearest trailhead (no problem, I thought, break your ankle the day of a marathon, shrug it off, and go do the race). I guess my guardian angel buffered my fall and the worst didn't happen. I was able to travel that afternoon in varying degrees of pain. It turned out to be only slightly painful on level trail, moderately painful on steep stretches, and unmanageable only when off the trail on rough terrain. As I hobbled along hoping I wasn't doing any permanent damage, but grateful I was able to keep going, I was reminded of Sparky Anderson's words of wisdom. The long-time major league manager was quoted as saying, "pain won't hurt ya," a line which now made complete sense. A few long soaks in ice water creeks helped keep the swelling down, but I still had doubts about my ability to climb up to Trail Crest and Mt. Whitney in the coming days. Subsequent X-rays revealed that there was indeed a break. Fortunately, my ankle was only sprained—it was my foot that was broken—which is why I was able to continue. I guess you could say that I got a good break. This is (to date) the worst injury I've had in the mountains,

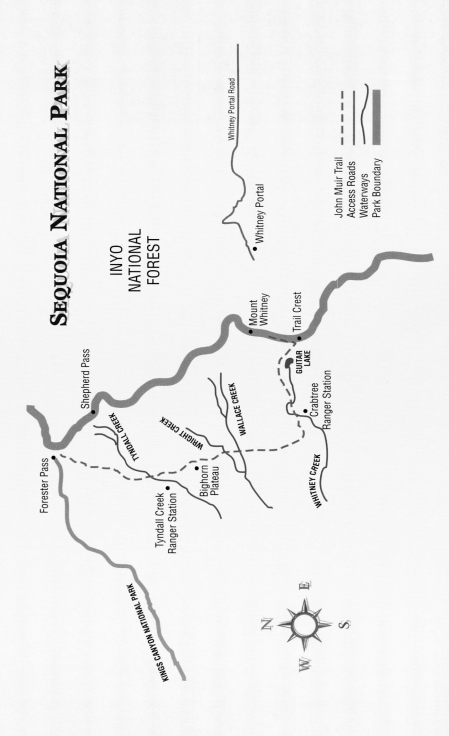

SEQUOIA NATIONAL PARK

INYO
NATIONAL
FOREST

Whitney Portal Road

Whitney Portal

Mount Whitney

Trail Crest

Shepherd Pass

GUITAR LAKE

Crabtree Ranger Station

WALLACE CREEK

WRIGHT CREEK

TYNDALL CREEK

Forester Pass

Bighorn Plateau

Tyndall Creek Ranger Station

WHITNEY CREEK

KINGS CANYON NATIONAL PARK

John Muir Trail
Access Roads
Waterways
Park Boundary

N
E
S
W

but it wasn't my last break of the day. You could say that all the breaks were going my way, as later that same afternoon I broke my fly rod. Ever have one of those days?

Tyndall Creek

Now, back to the trout fishing. The first fishing opportunity south of Forester Pass is an outstanding one. Charles McDermand, in *Waters of the Golden Trout Country*, called Tyndall Creek "One of the finest trout streams in the world" and said "...we found upper Tyndall to be a fly fisherman's dream come true." He reported catching golden and brook trout to 11 inches. A half century later, nothing has changed on Tyndall Creek; there are still plenty of golden and brook trout that reach 11 inches in this gorgeous water. I found the bigger fish downstream from the trail crossing in the pockets and holes. Upstream in the meadow, the trout aren't as large, but the casting is easier and the setting is hard to beat. As you stroll upstream through the meadow flipping dry flies to hungry goldens, you can look at the Kings-Kern Divide in front of you, the Great Western Divide to your left, and the 13,000- and 14,000-foot peaks of the Sierra Crest to your right. There can't be many trout streams anywhere that provide a background as dramatic as this. These are attractive trout in a spectacular area, and they are large for creek-dwelling goldens.

Tyndall offers enjoyable angling, and is a true gem of a high Sierra creek, but I'm not ready to crown it with "finest in the world" status. As much as I

Tyndall Creek at the base of the Kings—Kern Divide. "One of the finest trout streams in the world," says Charles McDermand, author of Waters of the Golden Trout Country.

appreciate beauty in the fish I catch, and the places I catch them, and rank those attributes high when judging a fishing spot, I'd like to think that there is a trout stream or two in the world that combines great scenery with wild colorful trout that run a little bigger. I will say that Tyndall surely is one of the best *high-elevation* trout streams in the country. I can't think of another one at a similar elevation (10,800) that offers so much. If you like stream fishing with dry flies for good-sized golden trout at timberline, leave yourself plenty of time to fish Tyndall Creek—it may be your fly-fishing dream stream.

South of Tyndall Creek, you soon cross a tributary that flows from a chain of unseen lakes to the east. Skip those fishless tarns and continue on to enjoy the panoramic view from the Bighorn Plateau. Surrounded on three sides by the highest peaks in the Sierra, with an unobstructed view of them, it's hard to leave this awe-inspiring place. Many Sierra veterans call the Bighorn Plateau their favorite place in the entire range. If there were trout up there it would probably be my favorite as well.

Looking across the Bighorn Plateau at the Great Western Divide. The Bighorn Plateau provides a perfect platform for 360-degree views of the tallest mountains in the Continental United States.

Wright Creek, Wallace Creek, Whitney Creek

When you reach the extreme southern stretch of the trail, three fine golden trout streams await you. The "three W's," Wright, Wallace, and Whitney creeks, provide enjoyable angling (www.goldentrout.fun?). The first of the trio is nicely flowing Wright Creek, which houses throngs of 6- to 8-inch fish. In another mile you reach Wallace Creek, which has much in common with Wright. It also has a good head of water that's home to a dense population of goldens that reach 8 inches. If you enjoy fishing Wallace you can thank the Sierra Club members who planted it with pure goldens in 1909. In addition to being a fine place to fish, this is a great camping spot. The benefits include: solitude, a pleasant meadow surrounded by trees, and a nice golden trout stream—virtually your own private stream for as long as you choose to stay.

Soon after leaving Wallace Creek, you step over a tiny fishless tributary as you set out for the Pacific Crest Trail/John Muir Trail junction. The JMT follows Whitney Creek for a couple of miles as it leaves the PCT to begin the eastward climb toward Mt. Whitney. You first glimpse the creek near the Crabtree Ranger Station, and later get good views of it from the trail that parallels it from above.

Whitney Creek's tempting waters will likely lure anglers off the trail for the short scramble down to its banks. There is a variety of beautiful water here—meadow runs, swift pockets, and brushy, rocky plunge pools. Throughout it all, the golden trout are abundant, and slightly bigger than in the two creeks to the north, reaching 9 or 10 inches with some regularity. Whitney Creek could easily be overrated because of its well-known, glamorous name, but it delivers solid, entertaining fishing, so it deserves any accolades that come its way. More people fish it than other area creeks because it's right along the trail to Mt. Whitney. Still, there are so many fishable miles that it's unlikely you'll feel crowded when picking a spot. Solitude seekers will like the narrow gorge below Timberline Lake—a unique stretch of creek that doesn't see many fishermen, due to its rugged terrain.

Timberline Lake

Tiny Timberline Lake, which sits on a narrow bench between steep walls, abounds with small golden trout. The trail follows the shore closely, giving the hiker ample opportunity to see trout rising within casting distance of the trail. The trout are commonly 7 or 8 inches, and top out at about 9 inches. If they were any bigger, this little lake could get overcrowded with fishermen. As it is, there are enough trout to easily handle the amount of angling pressure the lake receives in the few short months it's accessible. Another built-in limiting factor that protects it from heavy fishing is the camping closure. There simply isn't enough flat ground around the shore to provide legal campsites. Just above the lake, the inlet creek is also full of small goldens.

Two at a time. Bright twin golden trout from Wallace Creek.

The view west from Trail Crest (13,480 feet).
An exquisite vantage point where you're likely to linger.

Guitar Lake

The final body of water on the JMT is a good one to end with. Superbly scenic Guitar Lake sits right at the base of Mt. Whitney at an elevation of 11,500 feet. Camping is allowed at the lake, and the trout are bigger than at Timberline Lake, so consequently, Guitar does draw a fair amount of angling attention. There are plenty of trout in the lake, but they are somewhat wary and selective. Guitar doesn't teem with fish like Timberline, which is the reason the trout are larger. A long, fine tippet used with small flies is usually required to consistently fool the goldens that reach the foot-long mark. Even the more common 9- to 10-inchers fought so long and hard during the battle, they had me fooled me into thinking they were 12 inches.

The fishing is good enough to stand on its own, but the location is what gives the lake its special character. It's a sight to savor, watching golden trout leap clear of the water chasing emerging caddisflies at dusk, while Mt. Whitney towers directly above, basking in alpenglow. Guitar Lake gives a fine send off to the southbound fisherman who is ready to put away the rod and finish the JMT with the assault on Mt. Whitney.

Mt. Whitney

There is a point near the top of the steep climb to Trail Crest where Guitar Lake really looks like a guitar and you can see how it got its name (although, strangely enough, I studied the Hitchcock Lakes from the same spot and they didn't look anything like Alfred). There are some dangerously exposed ledges

Trout Fishing the JOHN MUIR TRAIL

on this stretch of narrow trail, which is why pack animals are no longer allowed. If you were to meet a pack train in such places, there would literally be no-where to go but back down to try and find a wide, safe spot to let them pass. The view from the start of the Mount Whitney Trail is another impressive one in the series of unparalleled vistas that have been coming in rapid succession since Forester Pass.

I got a good long look at the scenery as I sat eating lunch while trying to decide if I would make the culminating climb up Whitney with a sore ankle (at the time, of course, I didn't know my foot was broken). For 45 minutes I debated about which way to go, and was at a stalemate until my watch and the approaching storm clouds forced me to make a decision. I very much wanted to hike the entire trail, and knew if I didn't crest Whitney now, I'd someday make a special three-day return trip to do it. On the other hand, I wanted to avoid risking permanent, or long-term damage to my ankle. I was also relatively sure there were no trout up there. In the end, my cautious nature and analytical approach to decision-making was no match for the tantalizing sign I was staring at, which read: "Mt. Whitney—1.9."

From the moment I hurt my foot up to the time I sat eating lunch at that sign, I had decided that I wouldn't even consider going up. I guess the magnetism that mountains seem to have was taking hold of me (I always thought it was only trout that had this intoxicating affect on me). I found myself leaving my pack and heading up the trail "only a little ways to check out the view, I'll turn around at the first sign of serious pain." An hour later I was reading the plaque on the summit. The moment reminded me of John Muir's climb of Mt. Rainier. While on a trip through the Northwest he wrote to his daughter about Rainier, "Guess I will not be able to climb to the top of it and the weather is not safe." In his next letter, this one to his wife, he told of how he changed his mind, giving us some insight into his passion for mountains, "Did not mean to climb it, but got excited and soon was on top."

The plaque on the top of Whitney reads: "Elevation 14,496.811 feet— Sept. 5, 1930. This tablet marks the construction of the highest trail in the United States. Begun in 1928 it was completed in 1930 under the direction of the

Looking west over the stone hut on top of Mt. Whitney.

National Park Service working with the US Forest Service." The view from the top was impressive, and is probably tremendous on a clear day, but there were so many clouds around I didn't get the full benefit of my labor.

I had left all my non-essential gear in my pack below, except my fishing rod, which I brought with me to the summit. Why the rod? Well, I wanted a picture of myself on top of the highest peak in the Sierra holding the fly rod I'd carried on the entire trail. I got the idea from the three men who were the first to climb it in 1873. They called themselves the 'Three Fishermen,' and called the mountain "Fisherman's Peak." The previous name—Mt. Whitney—won out over the name applied by the first ascent party. In honor of their achievement, and to wrap up my fishing research, I thought it was appropriate to take a picture of myself on top with my fly rod.

It's said that Mt. Whitney makes its own weather, so I wasn't surprised when it started to snow, driving me from the nearly deserted summit. It was peaceful, being all alone up there, but I decided 14,500 feet wasn't the best place to be during a storm—especially without my pack. On the way up I had met quite a few people coming down, but as the late-afternoon snow fell, the trail was empty and all was quiet except for the sound of my footsteps. There were a lot of foreign languages being spoken by the hikers I met on the way up, reminding me that Whitney is a world-renowned destination, and reinforcing my decision to go to the top.

When I got down to about 14,000 feet the snow turned to hail, and when I reached the start of the Mt. Whitney Trail (13,480 feet) the hail began letting up. Two hours earlier that same 13,480 feet had been the thinnest air I'd ever breathed, but now it actually seemed like I was back in the lowlands.

When I reached the spot where I'd left my pack, I had no problem concluding that going up was the right decision. I also realized that I've done a number of more strenuous, out-of-the-way hikes to check the fishing at lakes that turned out to be barren (a condition that I had strongly suspected before going). If you have any doubts about whether or not to make the climb, I think you'll feel a nice sense of accomplishment if you do it, and it really doesn't take all that much extra time.

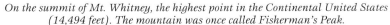

On the summit of Mt. Whitney, the highest point in the Continental United States (14,494 feet). The mountain was once called Fisherman's Peak.

HEADING HOME

Driving along Highway 395 on my way home from completing the last stretch of trail, it seemed to take forever to get from the town of Independence to Mammoth. I wondered aloud, "How'd I ever walk all that way carrying a 55-pound pack up and down mountains?" From the comfort of my truck it seemed tough, but during the hiking of it, the miles flew by, and I remember the days with fondness.

As I took off my pack for the last time, with the JMT concluded, I felt like I'd fulfilled an obligation. After all, many people went to a great deal of trouble in blazing, routing, and mapping these trails. Another group of people took the time and effort to plant fish in the region. Isn't it our obligation as Americans to take advantage of the extraordinary and unique public service that has been provided for us? Isn't it our civic duty to hike these trails and fish these waters as a way of showing our appreciation for those who worked so hard in giving us this gift? Maybe that's exaggeration, but in all seriousness, I do feel astoundingly lucky to live in a country where this opportunity exists. How fortunate we are that this massive, resplendent wilderness has been preserved for the common good and is accessible to anyone willing to put forth the effort it takes to reach it.

The enjoyment of body and refreshment of soul that the high Sierra provides is a priceless national heirloom, and the John Muir Trail links together its finest treasures. When I finished the trail I felt privileged to have witnessed some of the most magnificent scenery in the world. A hike through this extraordinary land is certainly a treat, but for a fisherman, to also find abundant trout along the way makes it seem almost too good to be true. I whistled my way down the trail, at times feeling like I'd covered miles where my feet hadn't so much as touched the ground, all the while catching gorgeous wild trout in places so stunningly spectacular and pristine that they seemed more celestial than earthly. If you've traveled the John Muir Trail you know exactly what I mean, and if you haven't, you're in for an experience to be savored—perhaps the experience of a lifetime.

EQUIPMENT NOTES

Fishing Tackle Recommendations

1. Carry waders. While not essential, a pair of waders can be extremely useful. Wading allows a fisherman to reach otherwise inaccessible water, giving wading fishermen a big advantage over shore anglers. You could wade wet, but waders will greatly extend your fishing hours, as the water is ice cold above 10,000 feet. Due to their size and weight, I would never consider carrying bootfoot, rubber, or neoprene waders on a backpack trip, but several companies make a nylon type that is lightweight and highly compressible. Many only weigh about one pound, and don't take up much room in a pack. I don't use waders at every river and lake I fish, but at the end of a trip, I'm always glad that I had them along.

2. Carry wading shoes. Waders aren't much good without wading shoes to go with them. The two best ultra-light wading shoes I know of are made by Orvis and Patagonia. At only 2 pounds per pair, they don't weigh much more than tennis shoes, and take up about the same amount of room. They are felt-soled, over-the-ankle, foldable, quick-drying, and comfortable. I also use these as a camp shoe when my hiking boots are drying out or my feet need a break from them. Their best non-fishing use comes on the trail when facing a wet ford. Felt-soled wading shoes are a step up from sandals, and two steps up from the tennis shoes that many hikers carry to avoid barefoot stream crossings. When attempting to cross a high, fast, cold stream with a full pack, the felt soles provide a safer and quicker crossing. I've seen people with tennis shoes, bare feet, or even water sandals, struggling and teetering across streams that were a breeze for my felt-soled shoes.

On occasion, I've worn both my waders and wading shoes while attempting to cross a high, cold, difficult river on a cold day. Many hikers are baffled and some even turn back when faced with this situation. Sometimes the extra weight of wading gear isn't just a luxury that allows you to reach more trout and fish in comfort, but can be an essential part of your hiking gear as well.

3. Carry a spare rod. It seems rather extreme to suggest an extra rod, and it's something I never considered until I broke the tip off mine while in the middle of a week-long trip, 25 miles from the nearest trailhead. I managed to use duct tape to reconnect the tip, which allowed me to make sloppy but passable casts, although setting the hook was a low-percentage proposition. I could cast short distances decently, but with a spaghetti noodle tip, I missed 90% of the strikes I got. The trout must have thought I was crazy. I imagined them saying to each other, "What's wrong with this guy, why can't he hook us?" I was probably an equally baffling sight to human onlookers. They must have wondered, "How can someone that is obviously competent at finding fish and getting them to strike, be so incompetent when it comes to hooking them?" Because I had experience with trout—reading water and choosing flies—I still was able to catch my share of fish, much to the dismay of passersby watching me slap the water and miss strikes by the dozens.

The next trip, I really felt prepared with an extra 4-piece rod tucked in my pack like an insurance policy. It took up hardly any room, and weighed just a few ounces, making me wonder why I hadn't thought to carry it in years past. I had, after all, broken two rods in the previous two years, but I viewed those as freak accidents since I had gone ten years before that without breaking one. Of course, on that first trip with the extra rod, my reel broke—which leads to the next tip.

4. Carry a spare reel. A reel is more durable than a rod, but I found out that they do malfunction. With the drag broken on mine, I could still cast, but I lost a lot of valuable fishing time stripping and untangling fly line—and lost a few fish as well. I've had reels last so long that I never considered carrying a replacement, but since I often carry a spare spool (with a sink-tip line) it makes sense to carry an extra reel instead of just the spool. The entire reel isn't much bigger than the spool, and the extra weight is a nice bit of insurance to have on a trip where the object is to catch trout. When I was 30 miles from the trailhead and looking at spending a week fishing with a broken reel, I would have been willing to trade anything in my pack for another reel.

So, besides learning that an intact rod is more valuable than a functioning reel, I learned to take an extra one of each when going on an extended trip by myself. If traveling with other fishermen, it's not as crucial, as you could always take turns in the event of an equipment breakdown. But, if fishing is the main purpose for the trip, I'd advise one person to carry an extra rod, and another to bring along an extra reel.

5. Carry more flies than you think you'll need. They weigh next to nothing, and don't take up any appreciable space. It's frustrating to spend days on the trail trying to reach a prime fishing spot, only to realize that you don't have the right fly when you arrive.

Recommended Flies

A good general assortment of flies would predominately contain dries in the size 12 to 16 range, and many of those would be attractor patterns such as the Royal Wulff or Humpy. General mayfly and caddisfly patterns like Adams and Elk Hair Caddis in the same sizes would also be useful. For sub-surface fishing, size 10-16 Hare's Ear, Pheasant Tail, and Bird's Nest nymphs would be a good start. Small Pheasant Tail nymphs (18-20) come in handy for imitating mosquito and midge larvae, so I'd want a few of those for the lakes. Throw in some larger Woolly Buggers (4-8) in a couple of different colors, and you'd have your core selection nearly completed.

The final components to this selection are the all-important terrestrial patterns. Terrestrials are often the only food available to the high-elevation trout, and they sustain the fish between hatches of aquatic insects. Black ants and beetles are common in the high country, and at times the trout selectively feed on them—especially at the lakes. My Sierra Bug is extremely versatile at imitating both, so I carry them in many sizes (12-20).

Besides throwing in other favorites, specialty flies, and oddities (remember, you can't have too many flies), the final terrestrial pattern is one I consider mandatory for all high-Sierra fly fishermen—the grasshopper. Hopper patterns are like American Express cards—don't leave home without them. I've seen grasshoppers at 12,000 feet up and down the mountain range. If you're like me, sticking with dry flies until they're proven ineffective, (and a few minutes beyond that point), using a hopper is a great way to extend your dry-fly fishing time.

Dries are always my first choice when fishing in the mountains; only stubbornly will I switch to nymphs. Nymphs aren't often necessary in the high country, as the short growing season and low insect population make the wilderness trout hungry opportunists. These trout are generally not too suspicious, but if they are, because of fishing pressure in the most popular spots, it's usually big spinning lures that have them spooked. In the heaviest-fished locations they'll often still rise willingly to something floating on the surface that looks natural, no matter how big it is. Yellow-bodied grasshoppers are the most commonly seen, and are imitated with a variety of hopper patterns (Joe's Hopper, Deer Hair Hopper, etc.) in sizes 8-12.

There is also a big orange grasshopper that lives at high elevations in the Sierra. My High Sierra Hopper in seemingly preposterous sizes (4-8), imitates these hoppers that grow as long as two inches. These can be just what the trout want during the times when there aren't any insects hatching, and these mouthfuls are certain to get the trout's attention when they hit the water.

The flies listed above would serve anyone well on a trip along the entire trail at any time of year. You could get by, and probably catch fish almost everywhere, with just a couple of dry-fly patterns in size 14, but there are plenty of times and places where you want to have a more rounded arsenal from which to choose. The emergency and first aid kit that I keep in my backpack contains a few size 14 dry flies, in case I lose my fly boxes. The emergency could either be that I'm hungry and need to catch trout to eat, or that I want to continue to fish for fun after losing the fly boxes in my vest.

Hiking Gear Recommendations

The following thoughts derive from lessons I've learned on the trail. Some were learned the hard way, others cheaply enough, but all were born of experience and may help you hike the JMT more comfortably. This is by no means meant to be a comprehensive list of gear recommendations, and much of it may seem obvious to experienced backpackers. Most of these thoughts were taken from the notes I made in my journal while sitting at a campfire somewhere on the trail. Many were meant as reminders to myself for future trips, while others were specifically geared to share with others. These bits of insight, modest as they may be, could be of minor use to one person, while saving the trip for another.

1. Carry enough food. This book isn't meant to be a menu guide, allowing a hiker to know where to get fresh trout all along the trail. I didn't title the book, "*How to Eat Your Fill on the John Muir Trail, Without Carrying Any Food.*" I release all my fish, and hope that the reader does too.

When I first started fishing the high country it was with spinning gear 25 years ago. Between trips, my brother and I would think of ways to reduce the weight of our packs. We thought we could get away with carrying less food by eating our catch. As our fishing ability increased, the amount of food that we carried decreased. Each trip saw us carrying less food until the time we decided we'd carry next to nothing and rely completely on our angling skills to fill our stomachs. Let me tell you, the lone 8-inch trout we caught on that 4-day trip sure tasted good. Our energy reserves were a little low on the hike out after skipping lunch the previous day, eating a dinner that consisted of a handful of sunflower seeds, and splitting our last granola bar for breakfast. We just about cleaned out the grocery supplies at the trailhead store when we finally stumbled in late that afternoon. I now prefer to bring enough food to maintain comfort, and leave the survival food gathering for real emergencies.

2. Wear polyester. By precipitation or (more often) by sweat, your clothes are going to get wet at some point. Polyester fabrics dry quickly, are light weight, and are extremely warm. The denim blue jeans and cotton T-shirt that are so comfortable to wear around town can be a nuisance, or even a hazard, in the backcountry. I once slipped badly while rock-hopping along a river at 10,000 feet on a cold day, and despite my waders, I ended up thoroughly soaking my clothes. Instead of a time-consuming or hypothermia-inducing incident, because I was wearing polyester, I just took off my clothes and hung them in the wind to dry while I sat by a small fire and ate lunch. It wasn't long before the clothes were dry and I was back on the river casting for golden trout.

3. Carry spares of essential items (especially lightweight items). If a flashlight is essential, carry two small ones rather than one big one. Also, carry an extra flashlight and batteries, not just extra batteries. If you lose or break your flashlight, the extra batteries will do you no good.
Have more matches, in different places, than you think you'll need. Matches don't take up any room, are nearly weightless, and could save your life. John Muir's family worried about him when he went on solo mountain journeys without blankets. His response to their concerns was, "...will be cold a little at night but will not suffer for I know well how to use a camp fire."

An extra camera battery is something that often gets overlooked— even by hard-core photographers. If it's worth going to the trouble of bringing the camera, it's worth tossing in an extra battery. Most people bring an extra roll of film, but what good is all the film in the world if your camera doesn't work? You'd probably be willing to trade gold for a spare if your battery died as you had a big golden trout in the net.

4. Bring good rain gear. A waterproof, breathable jacket is essential for comfort. The importance of the waterproof component is obvious, but the breathability allows you to hike in the rain without getting soaked in sweat. This also increases your hiking range by allowing you to stay on the trail during a shower when others are huddled under a tree, or in a tent, waiting for the storm to pass.

A poncho would seem to be a good alternative—until you've worn one in a heavy storm. They are loose enough that you don't sweat too much because air circulates underneath, but they're difficult to put on over a full pack (especially when you're alone). That looseness is their major drawback though. Ponchos are next to worthless in the wind, as they are so loose that they blow around and end up failing to keep you dry, since rain is often accompanied by wind.

5. Carry a bear-resistant food canister. You can no longer rely on the counterbalance method of hanging food to keep it safe from educated bears. The "All-Star" bears of the national parks can often overcome this method if it's not done exactly right. There are also bears that can get hanging food if it's done properly, and some, destined for the Yogi Bear Bruin Hall of Fame, that can get it even if it's hung in a way that exceeds existing standards. There are many places in the national parks along the JMT where bearproof food lockers can be found. I prefer to carry my own canister, as it gives me the freedom to camp wherever I choose, instead of being tied to the locations of the lockers. But, many hikers would rather have a lighter pack (the canisters weigh about 3 pounds) than the extra freedom.

Location of Food Lockers on the John Muir Trail (N-S)
Yosemite National Park: Yosemite Valley, Little Yosemite Valley, Tuolumne Meadows

Kings Canyon National Park: Woods Creek Crossing, Arrowhead Lake, Lower Rae Lake, Middle Rae Lake, Charlotte Lake, Vidette Meadow, 9900-foot Elevation/JMT, Center Basin Trail

Sequoia National Park: Tyndall Creek, Wallace Creek, Lower Crabtree Meadow, Crabtree Ranger Station

6. Carry a hiking pole. The trails are starting to look like ski slopes as more hikers are using poles. For my taste, carrying two poles is cumbersome, especially when combined with the fishing rod that is often in my hands. I don't find the hiking poles to be of any advantage on most sections of trail, but they do have their moments. They can be helpful when crossing creeks and rivers, and can be a valuable safeguard when encountering snow and ice. So, for the times when they are useful, I like to carry a single, telescoping pole in my pack, which keeps my hands free while hiking the bulk of the trail. A single pole weighs about 1 pound, and will collapse down to about 24 inches—so it can be stored with your multi-piece fishing rod.

These poles make even more sense for a fisherman, because they can serve as a wading staff too. I've sometimes arrived at a backcountry river and wished I had my wading staff to help me negotiate its strong current while fishing. I seldom bring my wooden wading staff on long hikes because of the inconvenience, but I feel uncomfortable fishing a river without a staff. The dual uses for the telescoping pole have made it a standard piece of equipment for my pack, and it has even replaced my wooden staff on rivers close to the road because of its lightweight, compact convenience.

Hiking Tips

1. Expect less hiking efficiency at high elevations. It's important to know your hiking pace so you can plan your day and estimate where you are at any given time. But your pace can change based on the thickness of the air, not just on the difficulty of the terrain. I used to figure my pace at 20 minutes per mile on a level trail with a full pack, plus 2 minutes per 100 feet of climbing. I used this formula with great accuracy for many years while hiking all over Yosemite. When I got to the higher southern Sierra, I found I had to adjust the formula based on elevation. The old formula only applied to elevations up to 10,000 feet, but I had to add more time for climbing when at a higher elevation. My revision allowed 3 minutes for every 100 feet climbed when above 10,000 feet even after being fully acclimated. This seemed to be about right until I got to the southern end of the JMT and the highest mountains in the Sierra where the air is really thin. The 3 minutes per 100 feet applied between elevations of 10,000-12,000 feet, but I now add 4 extra minutes when above 12,000 feet, which occurs only at Forester Pass and Mt. Whitney.

   It's important to check your pace under actual backpacking conditions. Walking city streets at sea level without a pack isn't reliable. After a few days of carrying a full pack, when I experience the luxury of taking it off for a day of exploratory fishing with only a day pack, I can't seem to slow myself down, and the miles fly by.

2. Drink before you're thirsty, eat before you're hungry, get warm before you're chilled to the bone, and rest before your exhausted. This has been said before, but it bears repeating. When you're on your own in the wilderness, you can't let your energy reserves fall dangerously low. If you go for a run or bike ride from your home, you can push yourself through cold, thirst, hunger, and past the point of exhaustion because when you get home you can find instant comfort. You just turn up the heat, grab a drink from the refrigerator, take a hot shower, toss something in the microwave, and then go to sleep in a warm, comfortable bed.

   In the backcountry, if you push yourself to the extreme edge, you may not have the strength left to find and purify drinking water, gather wood for a fire, cook dinner, and find a comfortable camp site to set up your tent. You need a certain amount of energy to warm your body once you're chilled, and that may not be possible if conditions are extremely cold, your gear is wet, firewood is unavailable, or you don't have proper clothing.

   John Muir, more than once, spent entire nights dancing a jig to keep warm while waiting interminably for the sun to rise and give warming salvation. He had extraordinary physical and mental strength, but even he still needed some reserves to make it to the dawn. Once it's lost, regaining your equilibrium can be a chore, so the trick is to know your limits and stay within them, leaving some energy reserves for accidents, miscalculations, and surprises—so common inconveniences don't turn into emergencies. If you are faced with an emergency that threatens your well being, the hiker who is rested, hydrated, well fed, and warm is the one who has the greatest chance at overcoming the challenge.

3. Wait out a big storm. This tip comes directly from John Muir. When discussing the time Theodore Solomons found himself trying to outrun a snow storm (in what is now called the John Muir Wilderness) Muir offered the following observations about Solomons: "was not a mountain man or...he would have had sense enough to hole in, in some sheltered spot, pull in all the wood he could get hold of, and keep a fire going, instead of trying to make his way out in a storm." Later, Solomons himself agreed with that assessment, saying "I often wondered why I had not had the sense to wait out that storm..." Sometimes people do things in the heat of the moment that they know they shouldn't do, because of fear and panic, or just poor judgment caused by sloppy thinking and overconfidence. It can take more courage to sit and wait indefinitely in a lonely, cold spot than to run for safety, but running could also cost you your life, as it nearly did Theodore Solomons.

4. Cross difficult streams without your pack. If you face an uncertain wet ford on a big river or creek, leave your pack on the bank and scout out a route first. Once a suitable crossing is found you can go back for your pack and cross in a direct manner with the added experience of having done it before (twice before, since you crossed and came back). It will seem old hat the third time, which is good, because the pack makes balance much more difficult.

On small creeks that require a long jump to clear, it's a good idea to jump without your pack, especially if the creek is big enough that it would be dangerous if you were to fall in. After determining with certainty that you'll be able to follow, take off your pack and give it a good heave to the far bank (taking care to remove breakable objects such as unprotected fly rods or cameras). You are then ready to make a longer and better-balanced leap to rejoin your pack on the other side. If you are traveling with other people, this becomes much easier, as you no longer have to worry about being separated from your pack if you can't make the leap. The first person jumps across without a pack, the other packs are thrown over, and then the rest of the group follows.

5. Consider the conditions when planning the time of day to cross major high passes. To avoid thunderstorms, get over passes early in the day—when the weather is more likely to be favorable. However, you may want to cross a pass in the afternoon if it's covered with snow and you don't have ice-climbing equipment. The snow is more likely to be crusty, icy, and slippery early in the day. In that case, crossing in the afternoon when the snow has been softened by the sun makes more sense.

FLIES FOR THE HIGH SIERRA

Adams

Royal Wulff

Yellow Humpy

**Sierra Bug
White Upwing**

**Sierra Bug
Orange Downwing**

Elk Hair Caddis

High Sierra Hopper
(see recipe on page 95)

Deer Hair Hopper

Bird's Nest

**Pheasant Tail
Nymph**

**Gold Ribbed
Hare's Ear**

Woolly Bugger

APPENDICES

Thoughts on Going Light Versus Traveling Heavy

Like most backpackers, I'm always looking for ways to reduce the weight of my pack. My well-meaning, non-fishing friends have made some suggestions that I won't consider, such as leaving behind the waders, wading shoes, loaded fishing vest, fly rod, reel, spare rod and reel, etc. True, this would save me 10 pounds, but then I probably wouldn't want to go.

Try as I may, when I go alone, and don't have the luxury of splitting the weight of mutual essentials (stove, cooking utensils, water filter, first-aid kit, bear-proof food canister, and tent) my pack still weighs nearly 60 pounds when it's full of food for a long trip. If you're like me, there always seem to be a million things to load into the pack. Between fishing and backpacking gear, I spend a lot of time checking and rechecking items the night before I leave.

When I'm loading my gear the day before a trip, I always wonder about John Muir's pack. The famous image is of Muir going on an extended trip to the mountains with only his jacket, a sack of bread, and some tea (I could never understand why he needed the tea). The reality is that he did carry a few more items than those, but he still traveled extremely light. My pack more resembles that of legendary mountaineer Norman Clyde, who longtime Sierra Club Director David Brower dubbed, "The Pack That Walks Like a Man." Clyde is one of the few people I've heard of that, like me, carried a spare fishing rod and reel.

There's a fine line between being prepared and being overburdened, and one that should be arrived at through personal experience on the trail. The occasional long hiking day that doesn't leave any time for fishing gives me a feel for what it would be like to hike the trail without much concern for fishing. I met a few different parties that were attempting to complete the trail in fourteen days—which works out to sixteen miles per day. That sounded like too much at the time, and still sounds like a lot even as I'm resting comfortably at home and not carrying a 55-pound pack.

Most of the through-hikers I met on the trail were going solo and seemed to be rushing; averaging anywhere from 12 to 16 miles per day. I understand that people have time constraints in the busy modern world, but it seemed that many of the hikers just wanted to get the trail over and done with. They seemed to view it only as an accomplishment, or a challenge, or, in extreme cases, even as a job. They certainly didn't seem to be enjoying themselves, appearing to be more concerned with making their daily mileage quota than enjoying the day and savoring the awe-inspiring scenery. I must admit that I probably don't look much different when I'm rushing to the next fishing spot, but at least I stop and enjoy the fishing to the utmost.

One example of the extremes some hikers go to is the guy I met while I was having lunch just off the trail near a little waterfall on Palisade Creek. He said he was doing the trail for the second time, and this time he wasn't going to pick up any food on the way. He was only a third of the way done with the trail (about 75 miles down, 150 to go) and already looked worn out. He seemed enthralled as he watched me eat my peanut butter and crackers, as if merely seeing food would give him caloric energy. He said he had plenty of food, but was just cautiously rationing it. He didn't give a reason for his attempt, but perhaps he was trying to be the ultimate JMT purist. He did say that he was exhausted from carrying his 70-pound pack, and admitted he would never try such a thing again. 'Going heavy' wasn't proving satisfactory to him, but he wasn't a fan of the other extreme either. He told of meeting a guy who was trying to do the trail in twelve days (eighteen miles per day with no layovers). This guy was a 'going light' fanatic who wasn't carrying a tent or a sleeping bag! True, he could rack up impressive daily mileage totals, but in the end he was just another hiker who didn't seem pleased with his gear selection. Apparently he reported, with much chagrin, that he honestly thought he nearly froze to death one night.

Before every backpack trip I always scrutinize my food and gear closely, trying to bring only essentials, but seeking to err ever so slightly on the side of caution and over-preparation. I like to have one extra meal with me for emergencies, and would probably bring even more if I wasn't sure I could procure trout for the frying pan if the situation demanded it.

As I mentioned, sixteen miles per day sounded like too much until I analyzed my own typical day. I usually plan for about ten trail miles per day, but that varies depending on the quantity and quality of the fishable water I expect to encounter. I've come to realize that ten miles with a full pack on, plus a full day of fishing is probably similar in total energy output to sixteen miles of backpacking without the added fishing component. Understanding this can be hard for non-fishermen or for stationary fishermen.

Often I've gone into work on a Monday morning, exhausted from a weekend fishing trip. A co-worker might inquire, "What did you do this weekend?" My reply, "I fished all day Saturday and Sunday, from sun up to dark, both days," would be met with, "Oh, that sounds great, you must be all rested and ready to get back to work." Outwardly I'd respond with a polite smile and nod, while thinking, "Actually it's a nice break to be back at work where I can rest up for next weekend's trip."

My typical backpacking day covering ten trail miles also usually consists of four or five hours of cross-country scrambling—climbing rocks while circling lakes, rock hopping, and beating brush along creeks—fishing all the while. Because I have so much fun fishing, it took a while for me to realize that it was somewhat of a relief to put the pack back on. As I hit the smooth trail again my thoughts would be similar to that Monday morning at work, as I'd think: "now I can rest and recover from all that fishing." I wrote the preceding while sitting at a campfire on the JMT after one of the aforementioned typical days, but added the following disclaimer the next day: "the above doesn't apply when climbing over passes—no matter how tiring the fishing is, it's easier than carrying a full pack over a major pass." Now I realize exactly the kind of energy that is expended on days like that, which explains why I'm worn out at the end of the day (most hikers rest during their breaks, I fish). A hard day of this kind of fishing would be tiring enough without even factoring in the ten miles of backpacking. But, because the fishing is so enjoyable, I never seem to realize the effort it takes until the day is over.

Inexperienced and under-conditioned hikers would be foolish to think that they could travel as footloose as Muir. In talking to backcountry rangers in Kings and Sequoia, they tell me that whenever a new 'go light' craze hits, they end up with more rescue calls for hikers suffering from exposure or injuries— both caused by being unprepared for the elements. If you have a great deal of mountaineering experience and are in excellent physical condition, then you can get away with cutting out some items that might seem essential to novices. If you are so inclined, everybody can do away with non-essential gear that adds only to comfort and convenience rather than to survival and efficiency.

Trout-Fishing With John Muir

John Muir (1838-1914) is considered to be the father of the conservation movement, and is considered by many to be the main reason we have national parks in the United States. It's very fitting that the spectacular trail, that bisects three of the countries finest national parks would bear his name. Muir was a naturalist and writer whose knowledge and love of the Sierra may have been unsurpassed. He studied the mountains as a geologist and botanist, but left his biggest mark when he wrote about the strong emotions he felt for wilderness and natural beauty. He captured the beauty he saw with his words, a beauty he appreciated so much that he wanted to share it and save it for others. His numerous books and articles about the Sierra were written with such eloquence and conviction that they convinced his, and future generations, that the mountains were worth preserving. He was one of the four founders, and the first president, of the Sierra Club, an organization that has led the way in preserving and protecting the Sierra since its inception in 1892.

Was John Muir a trout fisherman? Would he have been fishing as he sauntered along the trail that was completed and named for him after his death? Did he fish as he wandered the Sierra in the late 1800s? What did he think of the sport of fishing?

These are some of the questions I asked myself as I read his books, letters, and journals while I researched the history of trout fishing in Yosemite, for my book, *Yosemite Trout Fishing Guide*. Yosemite was his longtime home and always his favorite place. While hiking the Yosemite trails, and especially when wandering off trail through the backcountry, I would imagine what Yosemite was like years ago, in Muir's time, before the roads and other conveniences attracted all the people. It's easy to imagine these things when you're alone in the mountains. I would also wonder what the fishing was like, although I knew that the high lakes were mostly barren before fish stocking was practiced on a widespread basis in the latter part of the 19th century.

When learning about Muir, I tried to make him out to be a fisherman. Of course he'd be a fly fisherman so we could be kindred spirits, after all, we shared a love of wandering alone through the Yosemite backcountry. When I began research on my *Yosemite Trout Fishing Guide*, I scoured his writings looking for tidbits, hints, or anecdotes about fishing. He was such a keen observer of the natural world, it made sense to me that he would be drawn to trout-fishing. I came up with no definitive proof either way, but I strongly suspect that he didn't do much trout-fishing as an adult or he would have written about it (he did write of fishing as a child on his parents' Wisconsin farm).

I've talked to many of Muir's descendants, including three of his grandsons, and they all said about the same thing—they had no recollection of anyone, including their moms, ever talking about him as a fisherman (their mothers were Wanda and Helen, Muir's only two children). They also said that there is no fishing equipment that belonged to him in the family heirlooms (one of the grandsons I spoke to has been an ardent fisherman most of his life, so he probably would have known about it if there was an antique fly rod that his grandfather had left to the family).

The reason I became hopeful that he may have been a fisherman stems from a copy of a letter I found at my wife's parents' house. The letter was written to John Muir from Warren Olney (my wife's great, great grandfather) who was another of the four founders of the Sierra Club, serving as the Vice President while Muir was President. I became intrigued with the possibility of John Muir—trout fisherman—when I read the letter, dated June 19, 1894:

> *My dear Muir:*
>
> *...Please remember me to Mrs. Muir and say to her we expect a visit from her...I have about decided to spend the fourth of July week at a place called Fouts Springs...Said to be good fishing. Come and go along...I believe it is Stony Creek, heading in Snow Mountain that is the hiding place of the trout we are to catch of. Come!*
>
> *Truly Yours,*
> *Warren Olney*

I found no return reply from Muir, so I don't know if he went fishing on that trip, but just the fact that he was invited was interesting. Incidentally, Warren Olney was a fly fisherman, and his Hardy Perfect reel sits on the bookcase above my fly-tying bench, next to his first edition of Muir's book, *The Yosemite*.

As a child, John did do some fishing, and he spoke fondly of it a few times in his book, *The Story of my Boyhood and Youth*:

> *"We always had to work hard, but if we worked still harder we were occasionally allowed a little spell in the long summer evenings about sundown to fish..." "The very first pickerel that I ever caught jumped into the air..." "No wonder, then, that our two holidays were precious and that it was not easy to decide what to do with them. They were usually spent...on adjacent farms to hunt, fish..."*

During his adult life, in his many writings, he doesn't mention himself as a fisherman. Perhaps in his later years he did a little fly fishing when he was with friends who invited him to join them in their fun, but certainly if he was a real enthusiastic devotee, he would have written about it. Whether he participated or not, he did make some observations about trout and trout-fishing that give us an insight into his opinion of the sport. I think the following excerpts show that he thought highly of trout, and respected the sport of fishing, but he probably had other things to do that appealed more to him.

He wrote to his wife from the state of Washington in 1889: "In the pool at the base of the fall there is some good trout-fishing, and when I was there I saw some bright beauties taken. Never did angler stand in a spot more romantic, but strange it seemed that anyone could give attention to hooking in a place so surpassingly lovely to look at..." In *The Yosemite* he wrote the following about the Tuolumne Meadows region: "If you stop and fish at every tempting lake and stream you come to, a whole month, or even two months, will not be too long for this grand High Sierra excursion." His views on planting trout in the barren high country were positive, as in *Our National Parks* he wrote, "...now many of these hitherto fishless lakes and streams are full of fine trout, stocked by individual enterprise..." In that same book, he beautifully summed up his feelings about the sport, in what I believe is the most he ever wrote on the subject of trout-fishing:

> *"Soon, it would seem, all the streams of the range will be enriched by these lively fish, and will become the means of drawing thousands of visitors into the mountains. Catching trout with a bit of bent wire is a rather trivial business, but fortunately people fish better than they know. In most cases it is the man who is caught. Trout-fishing regarded as bait for catching men, for the saving of both body and soul, is important, and deserves all the expense and care bestowed on it."*

Whether he was a trout fisherman or not, I think his words capture the essence of why mountain trout-fishing can hold such an exalted place in a person's life.

Top 20 Free-Flowing Wild-Trout Streams on the John Muir Trail

The first time I hiked the trail I expected to find unsurpassed scenery and dozens of lakes and streams that provided good fishing. I wasn't disappointed, as the scenery and the lake fishing lived up to my expectations. The rivers and creeks, however, even exceeded my lofty expectations. I wasn't prepared to find such high-quality angling in so many places. The John Muir Trail links up a substantial percentage of the best free-flowing, wadeable, public wild-trout streams in California. All the streams listed below contain healthy populations of 10- to 12-inch trout, some have yielded to me an occasional trout in the 13- to 15-inch range, and a few sometimes hold browns of 20 inches. They are listed not in order of preference, but geographically, from north to south.

1. Merced River
2. Tuolumne River
3. Dana Fork, Tuolumne River
4. Lyell Fork, Tuolumne River
5. Minaret Creek
6. Middle Fork, San Joaquin River
7. Fish Creek
8. Bear Creek
9. Mono Creek
10. Piute Creek
11. South Fork, San Joaquin River
12. Middle Fork, Kings River
13. Palisade Creek
14. South Fork, Kings River
15. Woods Creek
16. South Fork, Woods Creek
17. Bubbs Creek
18. Evolution Creek
19. Tyndall Creek
20. Whitney Creek

As I looked over this list, I came to the realization that I could easily spend an entire day enjoyably fishing any of them. So, plan your trip with that in mind. If you think you want to hike ten miles per day and complete the trail in three weeks, be advised that you may want to add another three weeks so you can spend a full day on each of these gems. Of course, that still doesn't include a time allotment for the lakes...

Honorable-Mention Creeks

There are many more creeks along the trail that have good populations of trout, but the fish are not quite as big as those that made the top twenty. The best of the remaining waters (most of which contain golden trout) are listed below, again, from north to south. If you consider it worthwhile to fish for 8- to 9-inch goldens in small creeks, don't miss these:

1. Crater Creek
2. Deer Creek
3. Purple Creek
4. Silver Pass Creek
5. North Fork, Mono Creek
6. Hilgard Branch, Bear Creek
7. West Fork, Bear Creek
8. Sallie Keyes Creek
9. Senger Creek
10. Darwin Canyon Branch
11. White Fork, Woods Creek
12. Center Basin Creek
13. Wright Creek
14. Wallace Creek

These smaller creeks, with their correspondingly smaller trout, may not hold your interest for an entire day, but each would certainly provide enjoyable angling for an hour or two. Between the two lists, there are 34 excellent rivers and creeks to choose from in the 210 miles of trail, which works out to about one every six miles. The lesson to be learned is this: if you enjoy fishing moving water, give yourself plenty of extra time when planning your trip.

High Sierra Hopper

Hook:	Long shank, dry fly, sizes 4 and 6.
Thread:	Black.
Body:	Orange poly yarn.
Wing:	Dark moose or deer body hair.
Rib:	Black hackle, palmered and trimmed.
Hackle:	Black, one or two sizes small for the hook.

High in the Sierra, usually between elevations of 10,000 and 12,000 feet, I've seen a huge orange-bodied grasshopper that I've never seen anywhere else. The high Sierra's answer to the giant salmonfly, these hoppers reach 2 inches in length—providing a big meal for trout that are in the right place at the right time. They certainly command the trout's attention when they land on the water.

This fly isn't meant to be a replacement for other hopper patterns. Smaller yellow grasshoppers are more widespread in the Sierra at all elevations, but there are some spots where fish key on these big orange mouthfuls. So, you should carry patterns to match both types of hoppers when venturing high in the Sierra. If the natural is found in the vicinity of the lake you're fishing, this fly can eliminate the need to use sinking lines and weighted nymphs, by bringing big fish up from the depths.

Bibliography

Books

Bade, William Frederic, *The Life and Letters of John Muir*. 2 vols. Boston and New York: Houghton Mifflin Company, 1923,1924.

Beck, Charles S., *Yosemite Trout Fishing Guide*. Portland: Frank Amato Publications, 1995.

Browning, Peter, *Place Names of the Sierra Nevada*. Berkeley: Wilderness Press, 1992.

Cohen, Michael P., *The History of the Sierra Club*. San Francisco: Sierra Club Books, 1988.

McDermand, Charles, *Waters of the Golden Trout Country*. New York: G.P. Putnam's Sons, 1946.

Muir, John, *The Writings of John Muir*. edited by William Frederic Bade. 8 vols. Boston and New York: Houghton Mifflin Company, 1917, 1918.

Muir John, *The Yosemite*. New York: The Century Company, Inc., 1912.

Roth, Hal, *Pathway in the Sky: The Story of the John Muir Trail*. Berkeley: Howell-North Books, 1965.

Russell, Carl Parcher, *One Hundred Years in Yosemite*. Yosemite National Park: Yosemite Association, 1992.

Sargent, Shirley, *Dear Papa*. Fresno: Panorama West Books, 1985.

Sargent, Shirley, *Solomons of the Sierra*. Yosemite: Flying Spur Press, 1990.

Starr, Walter A. Jr., *Starr's Guide to the John Muir Trail*. San Francisco: Sierra Club, 1964.

Winnett, Thomas, *Guide to the John Muir Trail*. Berkeley: Wilderness Press, 1992.

Wolfe, Linnie Marsh, ed., *John of the Mountains: The Unpublished Journals of John Muir*. Boston: Houghton Mifflin Company, 1938.

Wolfe, Linnie Marsh, *Son of the Wilderness*. Madison: University of Wisconsin Press, 1980.

Reports and Bulletins

"Angler's Guides," State of California Department of Fish and Game, 1977.

"California Department of Fish and Game Fish Stocking Record 1930-1997."

"Sequoia and Kings Canyon National Park Fish Stocking Record 1944-1978." National Park Service.

"The Status of Fish Populations in 137 Lakes in Sequoia and Kings Canyon National Parks." U.S. Department of Interior, National Park Service, State of California Department of Fish and Game, 1977.

"Yosemite National Park Fish Stocking Record 1933-1979." National Park Service.